Z

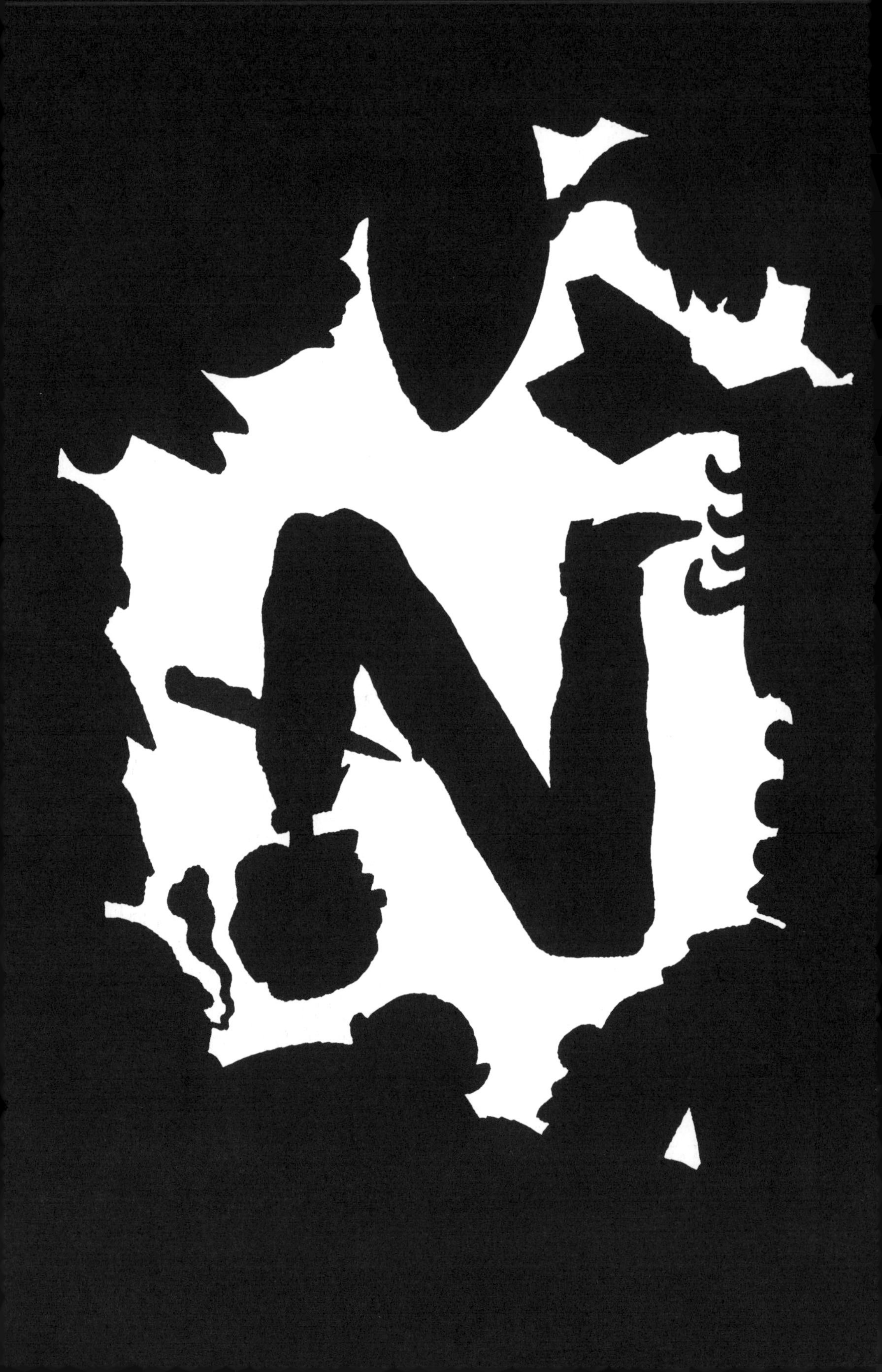

David B.

INCIDENTS in the NIGHT

Book One

Translated by
Brian & Sarah Evenson

Uncivilized Books, Publisher

Other Books by David B.

Epileptic

The Armed Garden

Nocturnal Conspiracies

Black Paths

Babel

Originally published as *Les Incidents De La Nuit* by L'Association.

Entire contents copyright © 2013 David B. & L'Association.

Translation © 2013 Brian and Sarah Evenson & Uncivilized Books.

Rights arranged through Nicolas Grivel Agency.

Design by Tom Kaczynski

Typography by Caitlin Skaalrud & Tom Kaczynski

Production assist by Dawson Walker

Uncivilized Books

P.O. Box 6434

Minneapolis, MN 55406

USA

uncivilizedbooks.com

First American Edition, April 2013

10 9 8 7 6 5 4 3 2 1

ISBN 978-0-9846814-4-0

DISTRIBUTED TO THE TRADE BY:

Consortium Book Sales & Distribution, LLC.

34 Thirteenth Avenue NE,

Suite 101 Minneapolis,

MN 55413-1007

Orders: (800) 283-3572

Printed in the USA

Table of Contents

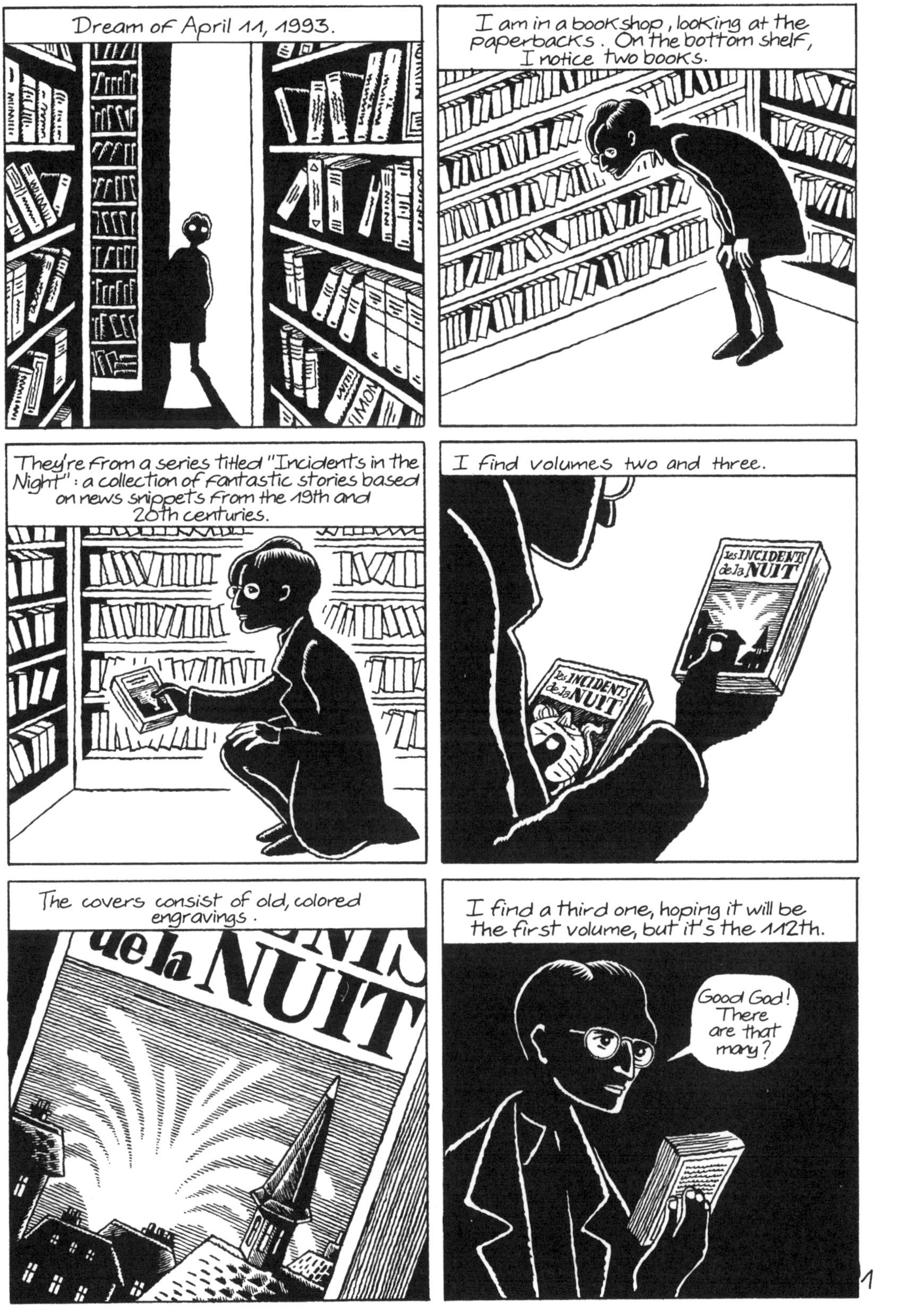
Dream of April 11, 1993.
I am in a bookshop, looking at the paperbacks. On the bottom shelf, I notice two books.
They're from a series titled "Incidents in the Night": a collection of fantastic stories based on news snippets from the 19th and 20th centuries.
I find volumes two and three.
Les INCIDENTS de la NUIT
Les INCIDENTS de la NUIT
The covers consist of old, colored engravings.
de la NUIT
I find a third one, hoping it will be the first volume, but it's the 112th.
Good God! There are that many?

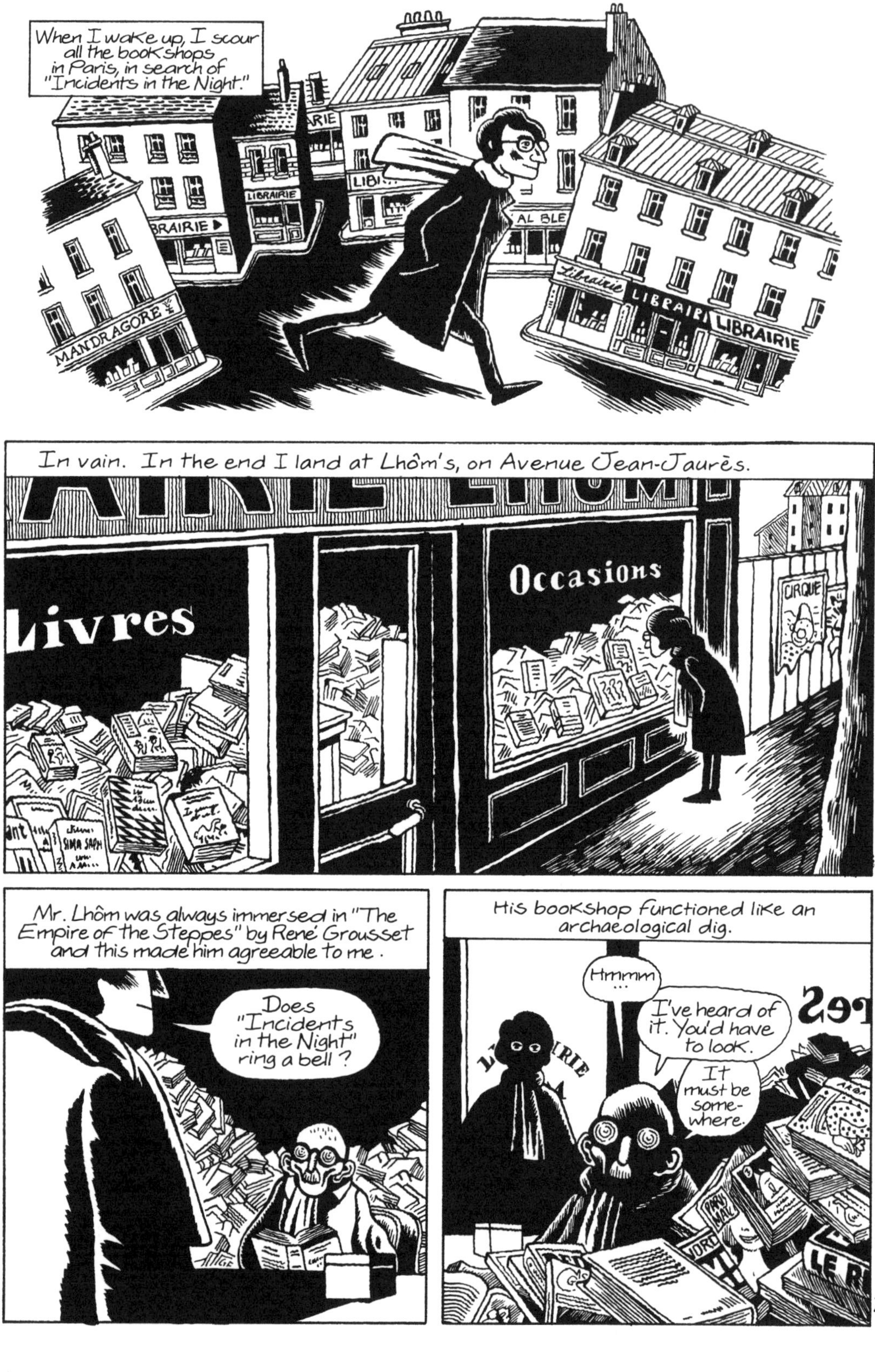

When I wake up, I scour all the bookshops in Paris, in search of "Incidents in the Night."
MANDRAGORE
LIBRAIRIE
Librairie
LIBRAIRIE
In vain. In the end I land at Lhôm's, on Avenue Jean-Jaurès.
Livres
Occasions
CIRQUE
Mr. Lhôm was always immersed in "The Empire of the Steppes" by René Grousset and this made him agreeable to me.
Does "Incidents in the Night" ring a bell?
His bookshop functioned like an archaeological dig.
Hmmm ...
I've heard of it. You'd have to look.
It must be some-where.

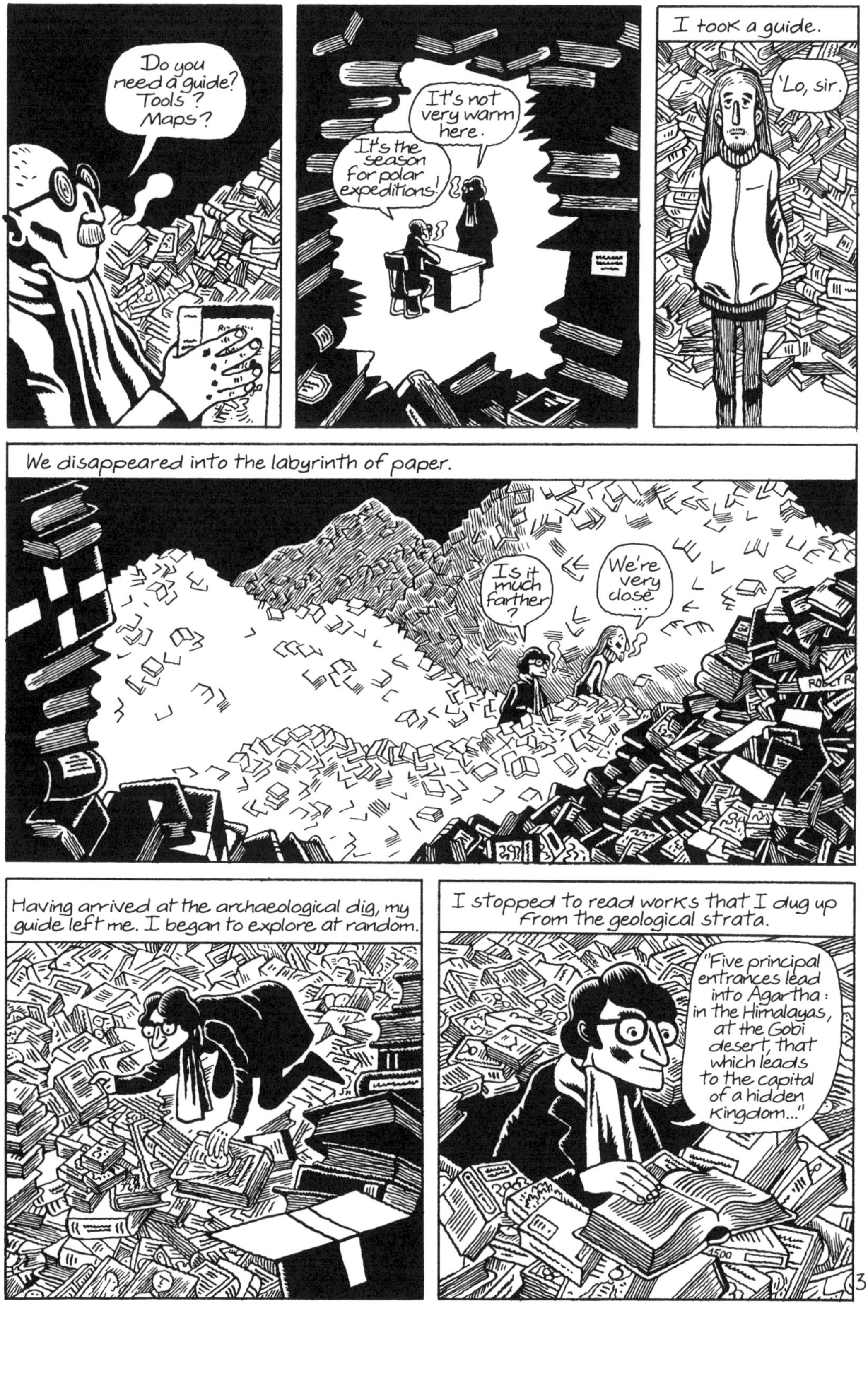
Do you need a guide? Tools? Maps?
It's not very warm here.
It's the season for polar expeditions!
I took a guide.
'Lo, sir.
We disappeared into the labyrinth of paper.
Is it much farther?
We're very close...
Having arrived at the archaeological dig, my guide left me. I began to explore at random.
I stopped to read works that I dug up from the geological strata.
"Five principal entrances lead into Agartha: in the Himalayas, at the Gobi desert, that which leads to the capital of a hidden Kingdom..."

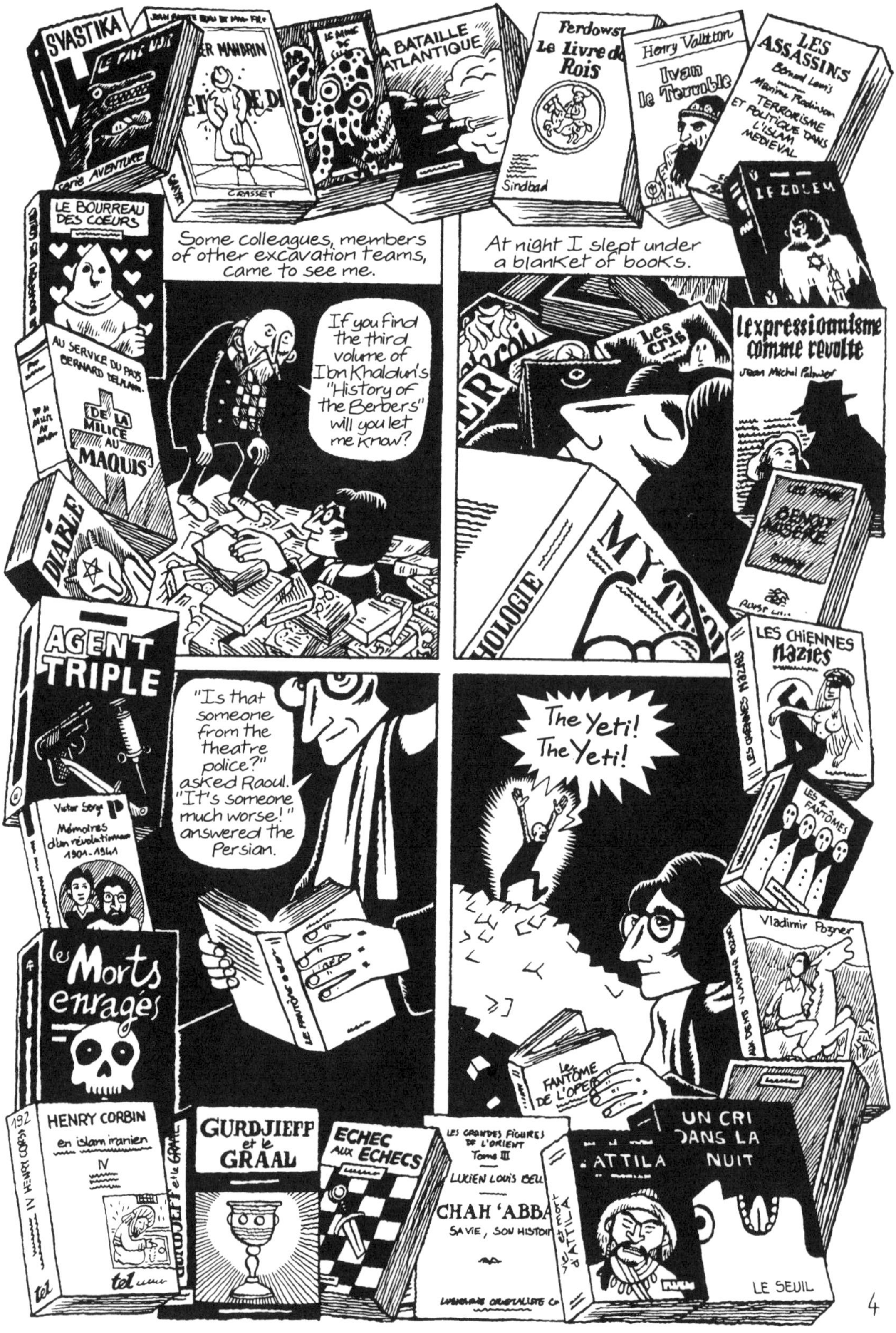
SVASTIKA
LA BATAILLE DE L'ATLANTIQUE
Ferdowsi
Le livre des Rois
Sindbad
Henry Valloton
Ivan le Terrible
LES ASSASSINS
Bernard Lewis
Maxime Rodinson
TERRORISME ET POLITIQUE DANS L'ISLAM MEDIEVAL
LE BOURREAU DES COEURS
Some colleagues, members of other excavation teams, came to see me.
At night I slept under a blanket of books.
If you find the third volume of Ibn Khaldun's "History of the Berbers" will you let me know?
AU SERVICE DU PAYS
BERNARD DELPLAIN
DE LA MILICE AU MAQUIS
DIABLE
L'expressionnisme comme révolte
Jean Michel Palmier
Les cris
MYTHOLOGIE
AGENT TRIPLE
LES CHIENNES nazies
"Is that someone from the theatre police?" asked Raoul. "It's someone much worse!" answered the Persian.
The Yeti! The Yeti!
Victor Serge
Mémoires d'un révolutionnaire 1901–1941
LES 4 FANTÔMES
les Morts enragés
Vladimir Pozner
LE FANTÔME DE L'OPÉRA
HENRY CORBIN
en islam iranien
IV
GURDJIEFF et le GRAAL
ECHEC AUX ECHECS
LES GRANDES FIGURES DE L'ORIENT
Tome III
CHAH 'ABBAS
SA VIE, SON HISTOIRE
ATTILA
UN CRI DANS LA NUIT
LE SEUIL

For a list of titles of the books on this page see Appendix I

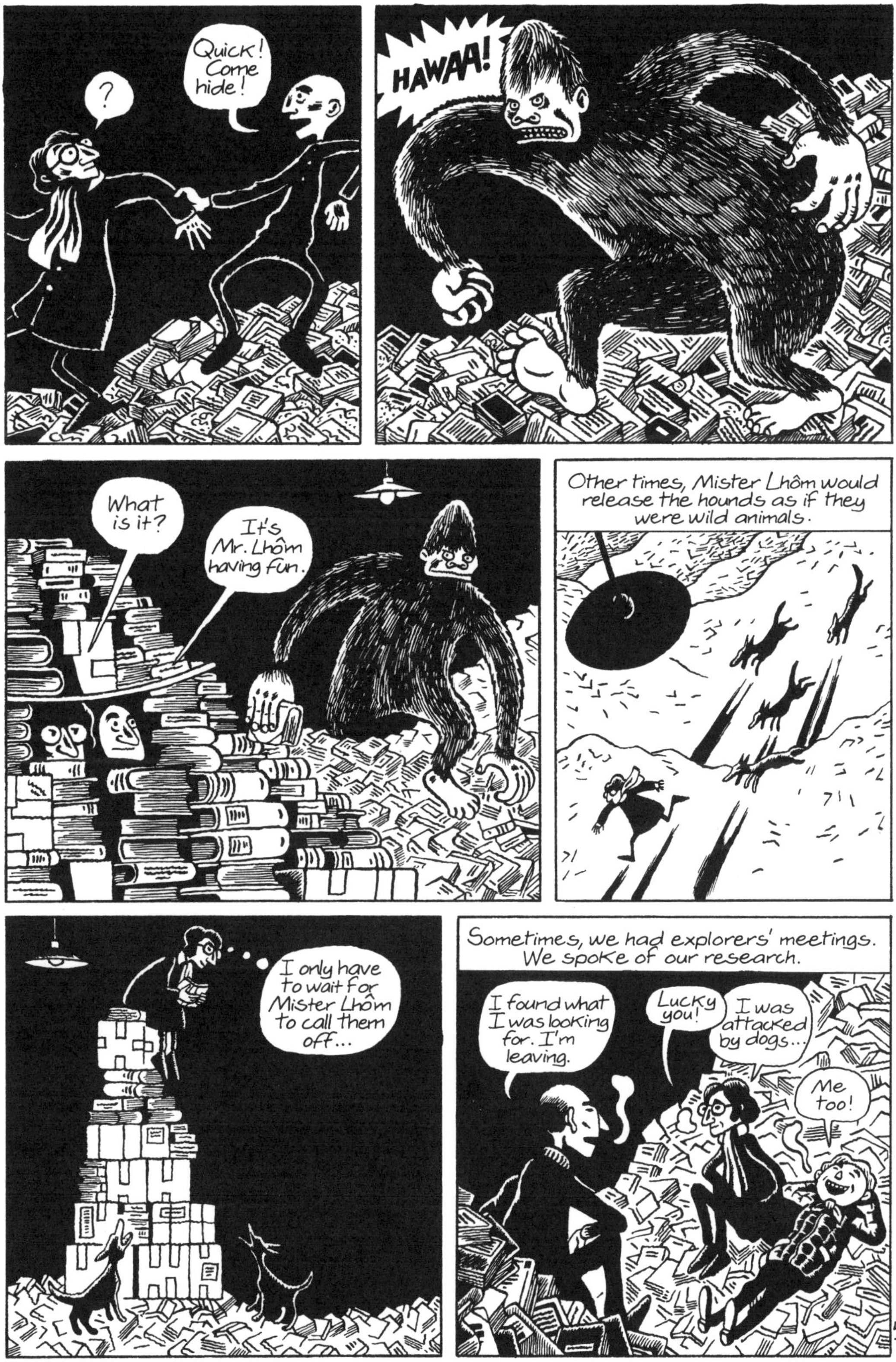
?
Quick! Come hide!
HAWAA!
What is it?
It's Mr. Lhôm having fun.
Other times, Mister Lhôm would release the hounds as if they were wild animals.
I only have to wait for Mister Lhôm to call them off...
Sometimes, we had explorers' meetings. We spoke of our research.
I found what I was looking for. I'm leaving.
Lucky you!
I was attacked by dogs...
Me too!

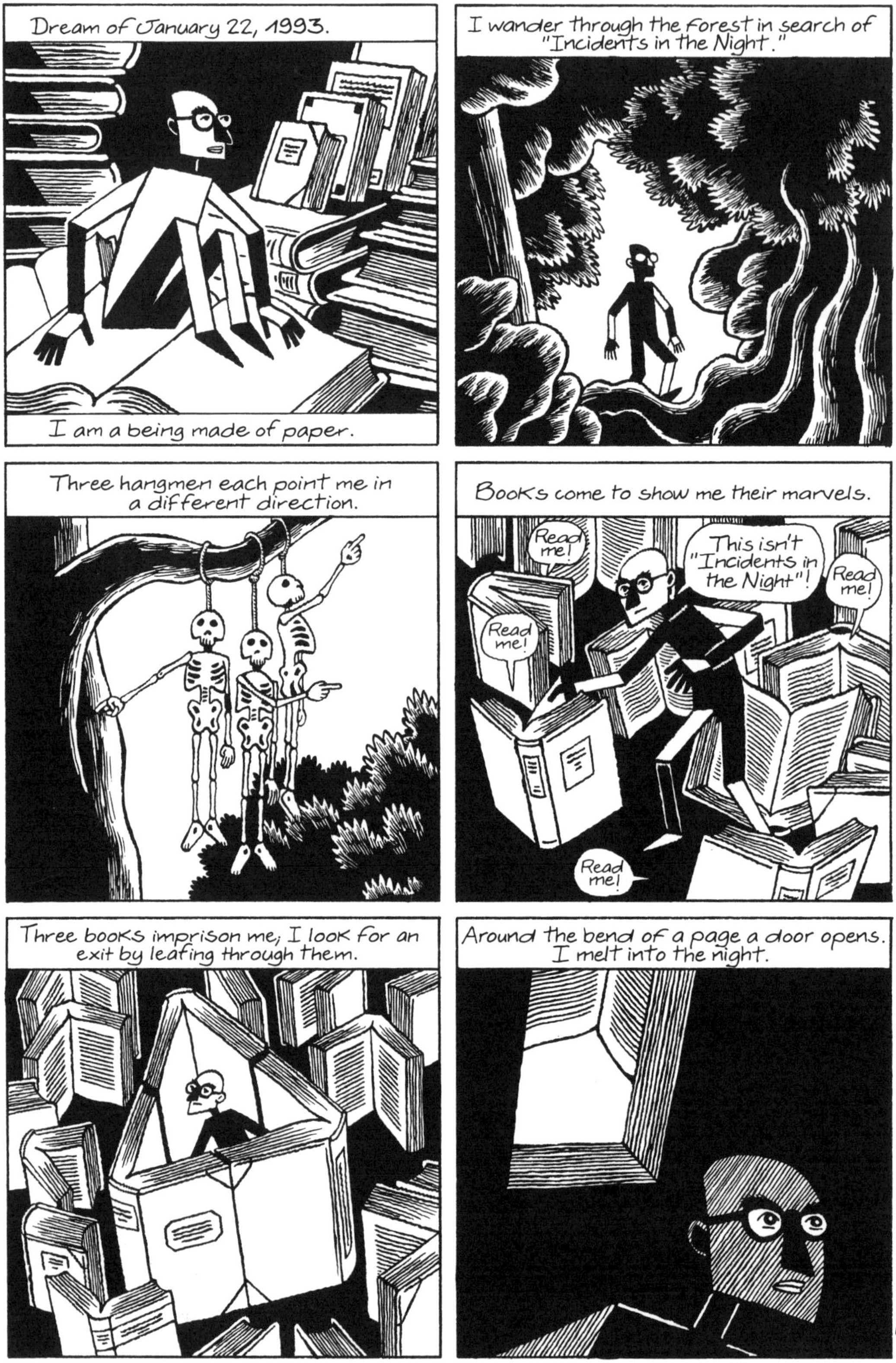
Dream of January 22, 1993.
I am a being made of paper.
I wander through the forest in search of "Incidents in the Night."
Three hangmen each point me in a different direction.
Books come to show me their marvels.
Read me!
This isn't "Incidents in the Night"!
Read me!
Read me!
Read me!
Three books imprison me; I look for an exit by leafing through them.
Around the bend of a page a door opens. I melt into the night.

After this dream, I was able to take on several forms according to my mood : I could be a shadow, a skeleton, a paper man, or else the human I usually was.

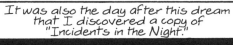
It was also the day after this dream that I discovered a copy of "Incidents in the Night."

At that moment, I felt very paper.

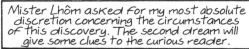
Mister Lhôm asked for my most absolute discretion concerning the circumstances of this discovery. The second dream will give some clues to the curious reader.

7

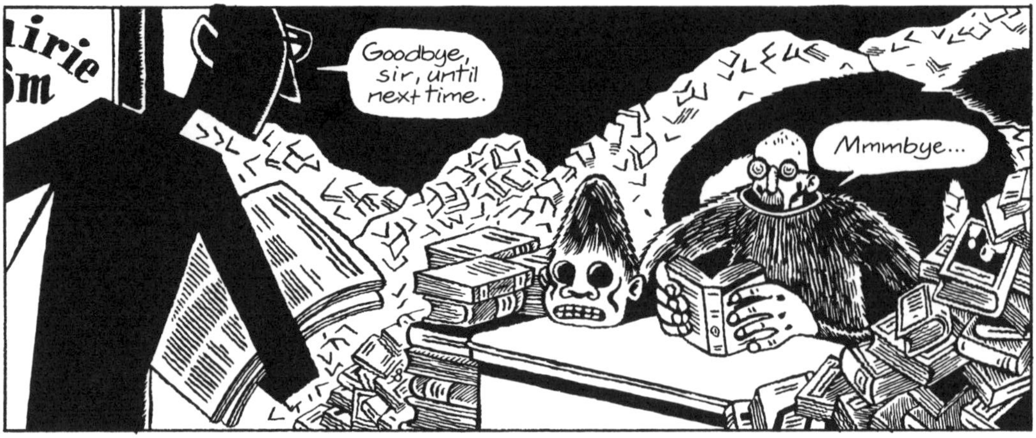

Goodbye, sir, until next time.
Mmmbye...

"Incidents in the Night" appeared for the first time in 1829. The title was placed under the sponsorship of the Angel of the Bizarre.

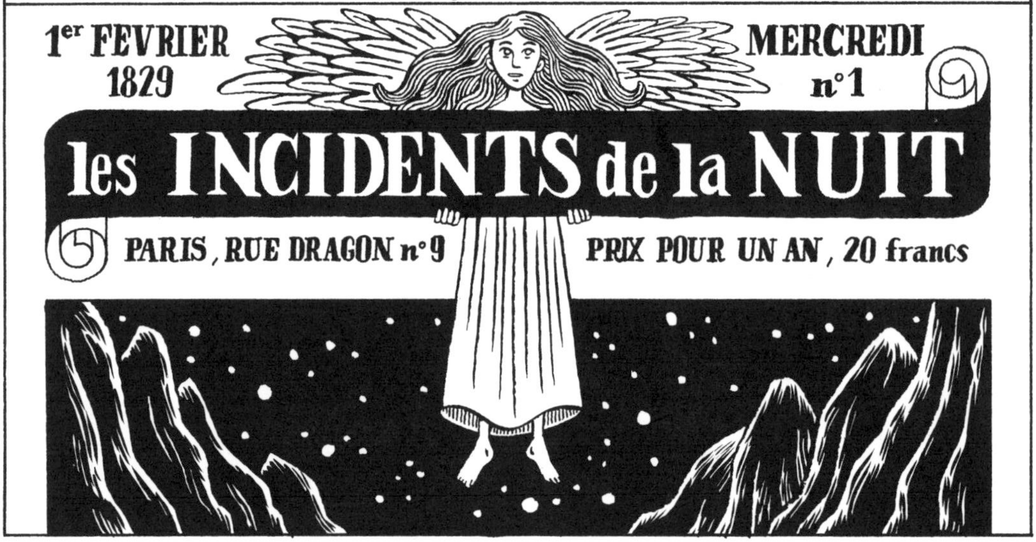

1er FEVRIER 1829
MERCREDI n°1
les INCIDENTS de la NUIT
PARIS, RUE DRAGON n°9
PRIX POUR UN AN, 20 francs

The founder of the journal, Émile Travers, had been disfigured at the time of the attack on La Sainte Farm at Waterloo.

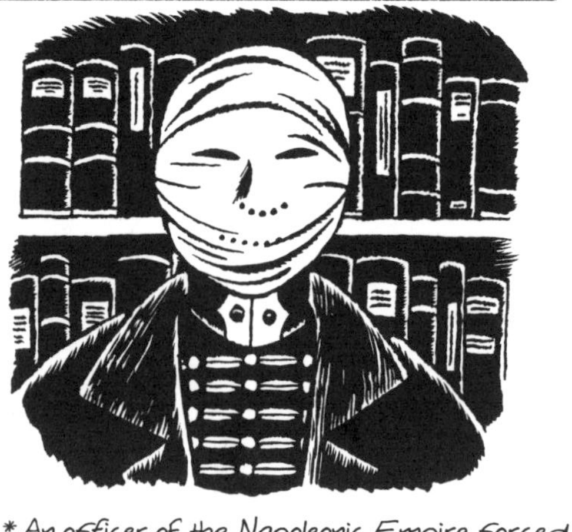

He was a dreadful man. He hung around in the city with a band of half-pays*, picking fights with royalists in the hope of killing them in duels.

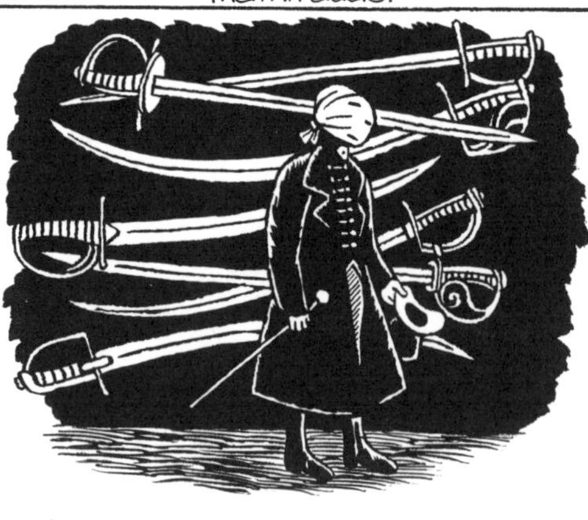

* An officer of the Napoleonic Empire forced into retirement after Napoleon's fall.

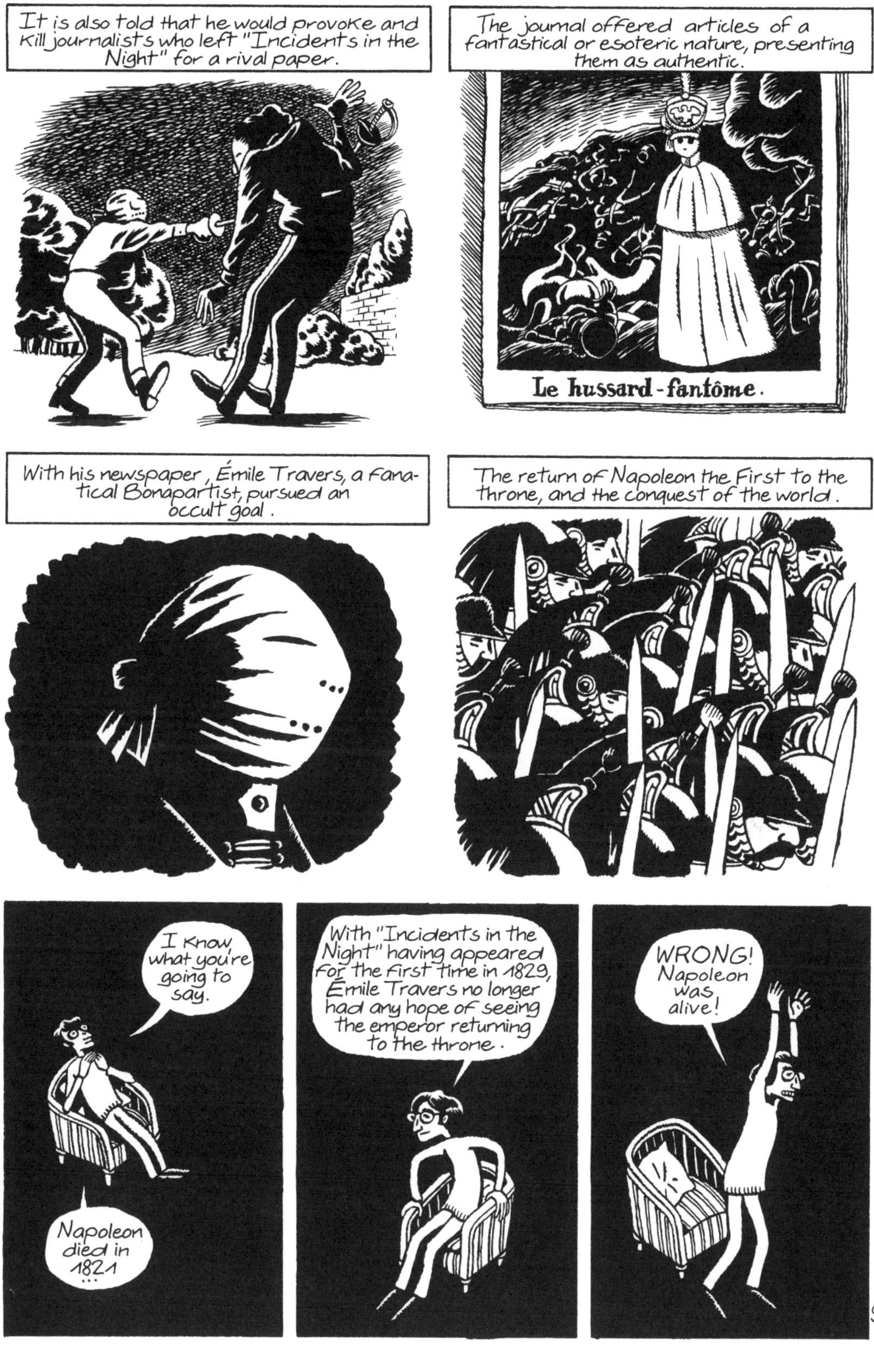
It is also told that he would provoke and kill journalists who left "Incidents in the Night" for a rival paper.
The journal offered articles of a fantastical or esoteric nature, presenting them as authentic.
Le hussard-fantôme.
With his newspaper, Émile Travers, a fanatical Bonapartist, pursued an occult goal.
The return of Napoleon the First to the throne, and the conquest of the world.
I know what you're going to say.
Napoleon died in 1821...
With "Incidents in the Night" having appeared for the first time in 1829, Émile Travers no longer had any hope of seeing the emperor returning to the throne.
WRONG! Napoleon was alive!

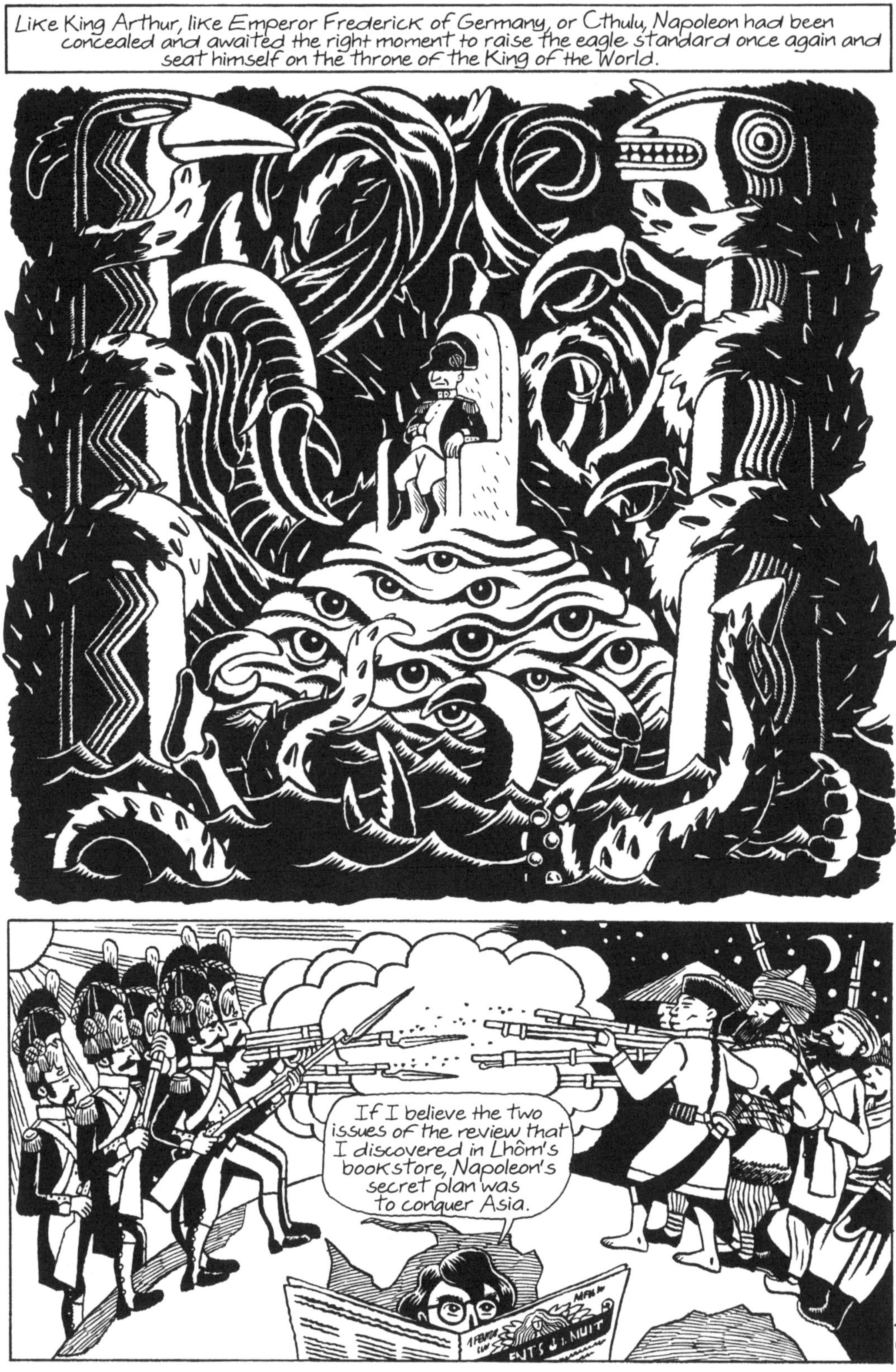
Like King Arthur, like Emperor Frederick of Germany, or Cthulu, Napoleon had been concealed and awaited the right moment to raise the eagle standard once again and seat himself on the throne of the King of the World.
If I believe the two issues of the review that I discovered in Lhôm's bookstore, Napoleon's secret plan was to conquer Asia.

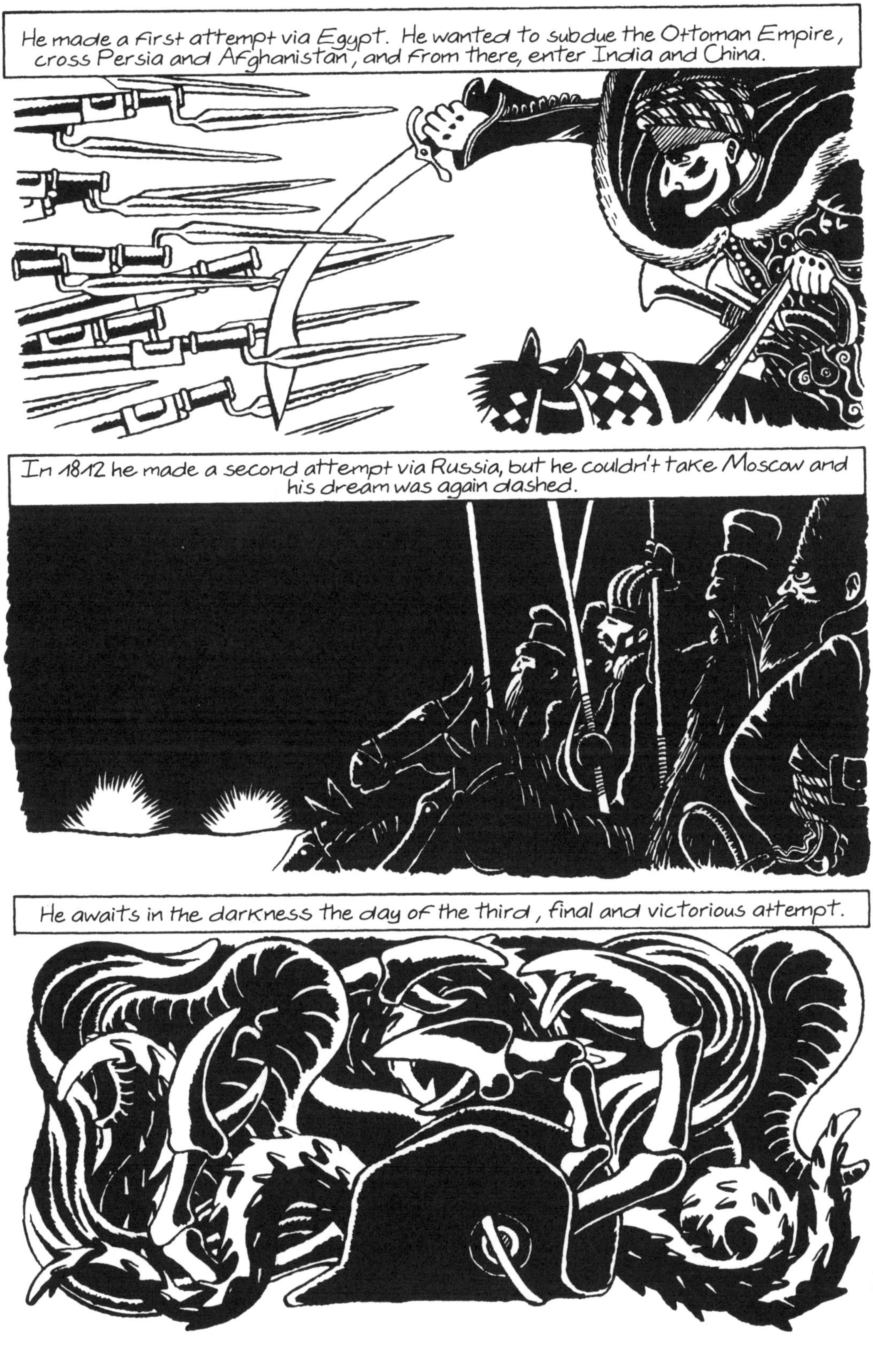
He made a first attempt via Egypt. He wanted to subdue the Ottoman Empire, cross Persia and Afghanistan, and from there, enter India and China.
In 1812 he made a second attempt via Russia, but he couldn't take Moscow and his dream was again dashed.
He awaits in the darkness the day of the third, final and victorious attempt.

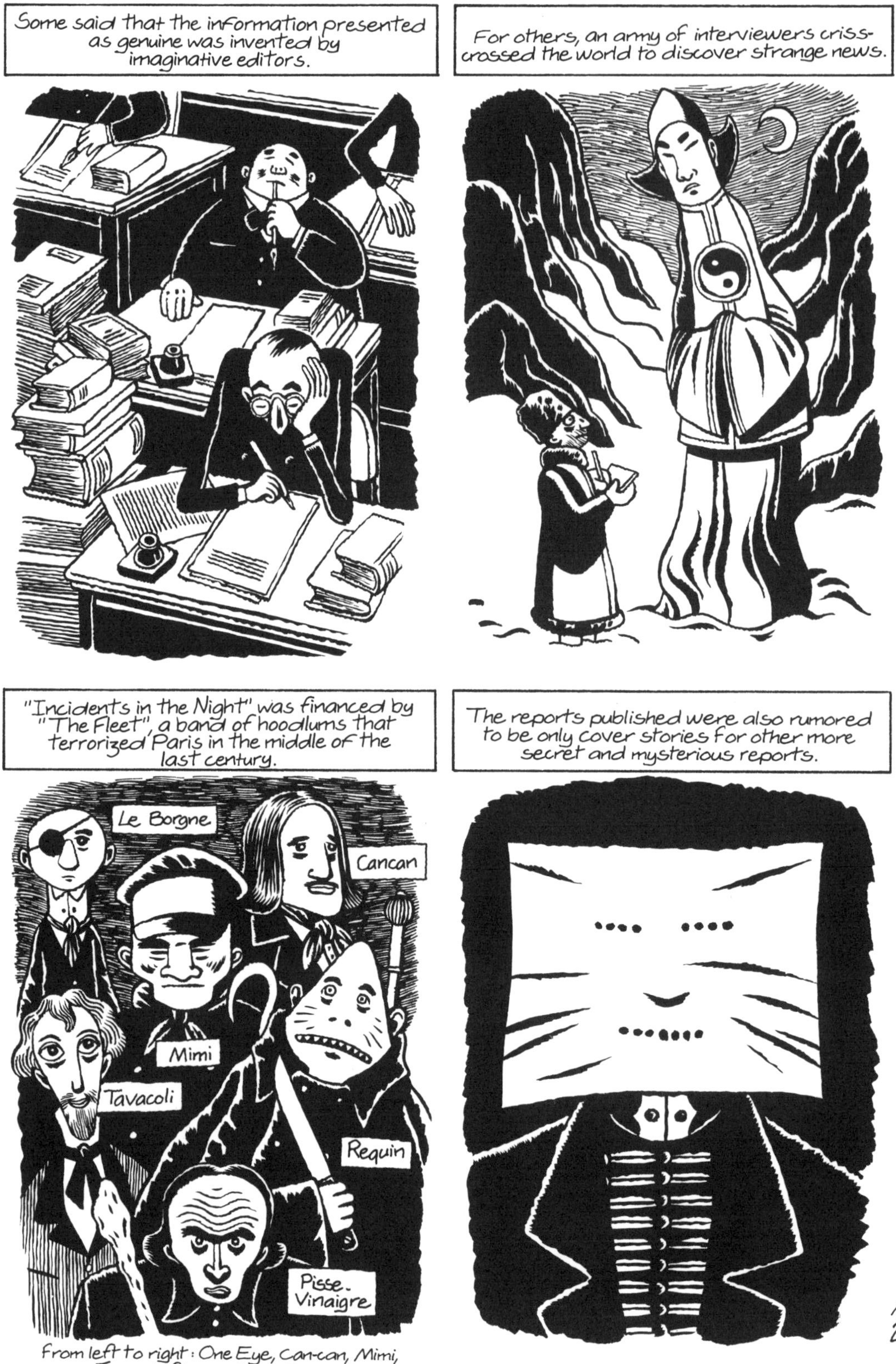
Some said that the information presented as genuine was invented by imaginative editors.
For others, an army of interviewers criss-crossed the world to discover strange news.
"Incidents in the Night" was financed by "The Fleet", a band of hoodlums that terrorized Paris in the middle of the last century.
Le Borgne
Cancan
Mimi
Tavacoli
Requin
Pisse. Vinaigre
The reports published were also rumored to be only cover stories for other more secret and mysterious reports.

From left to right: One Eye, Can-can, Mimi, Tavacoli, Shark, Sour-Puss

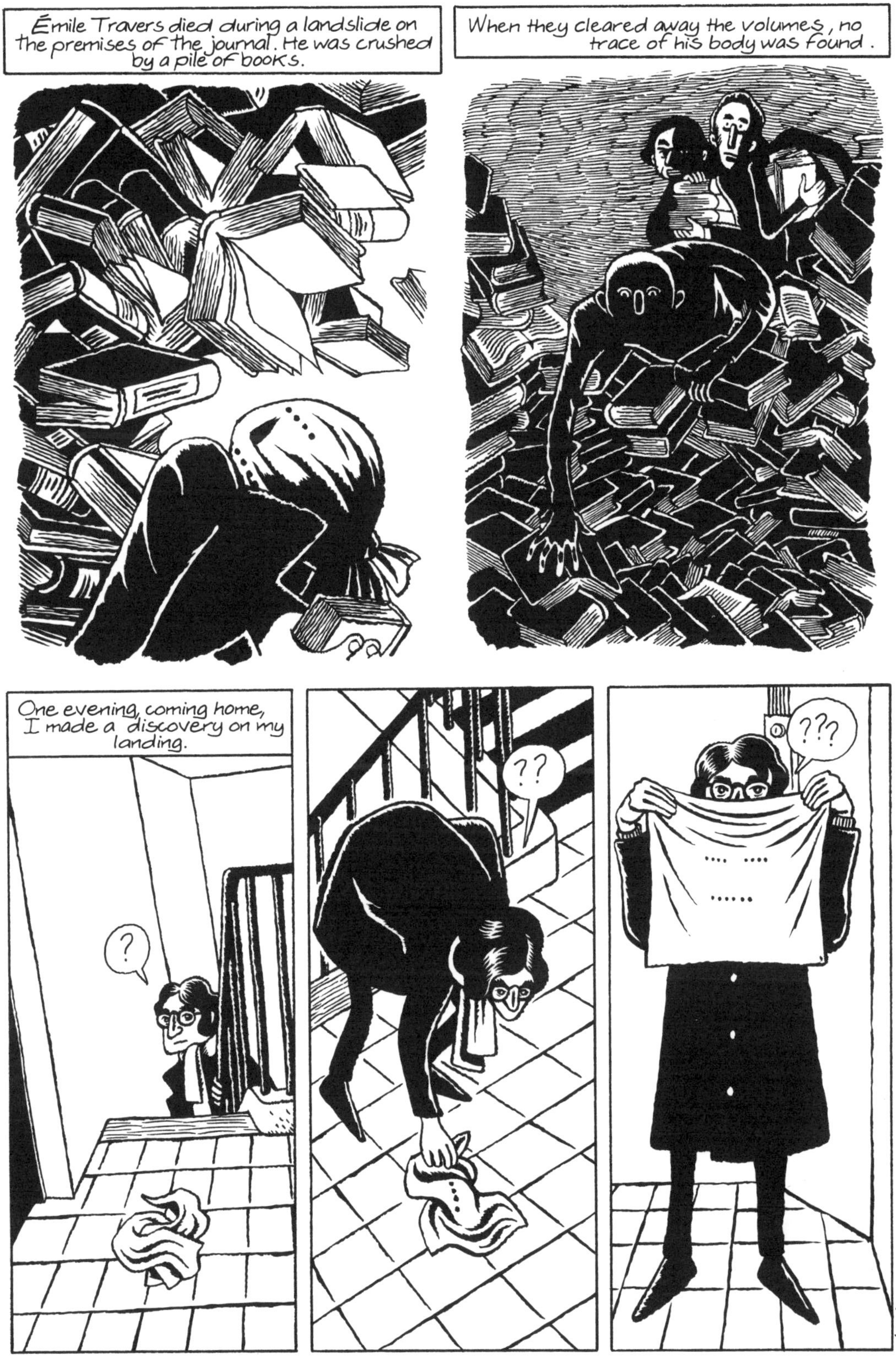
Émile Travers died during a landslide on the premises of the journal. He was crushed by a pile of books.
When they cleared away the volumes, no trace of his body was found.
One evening, coming home, I made a discovery on my landing.
?
??
???

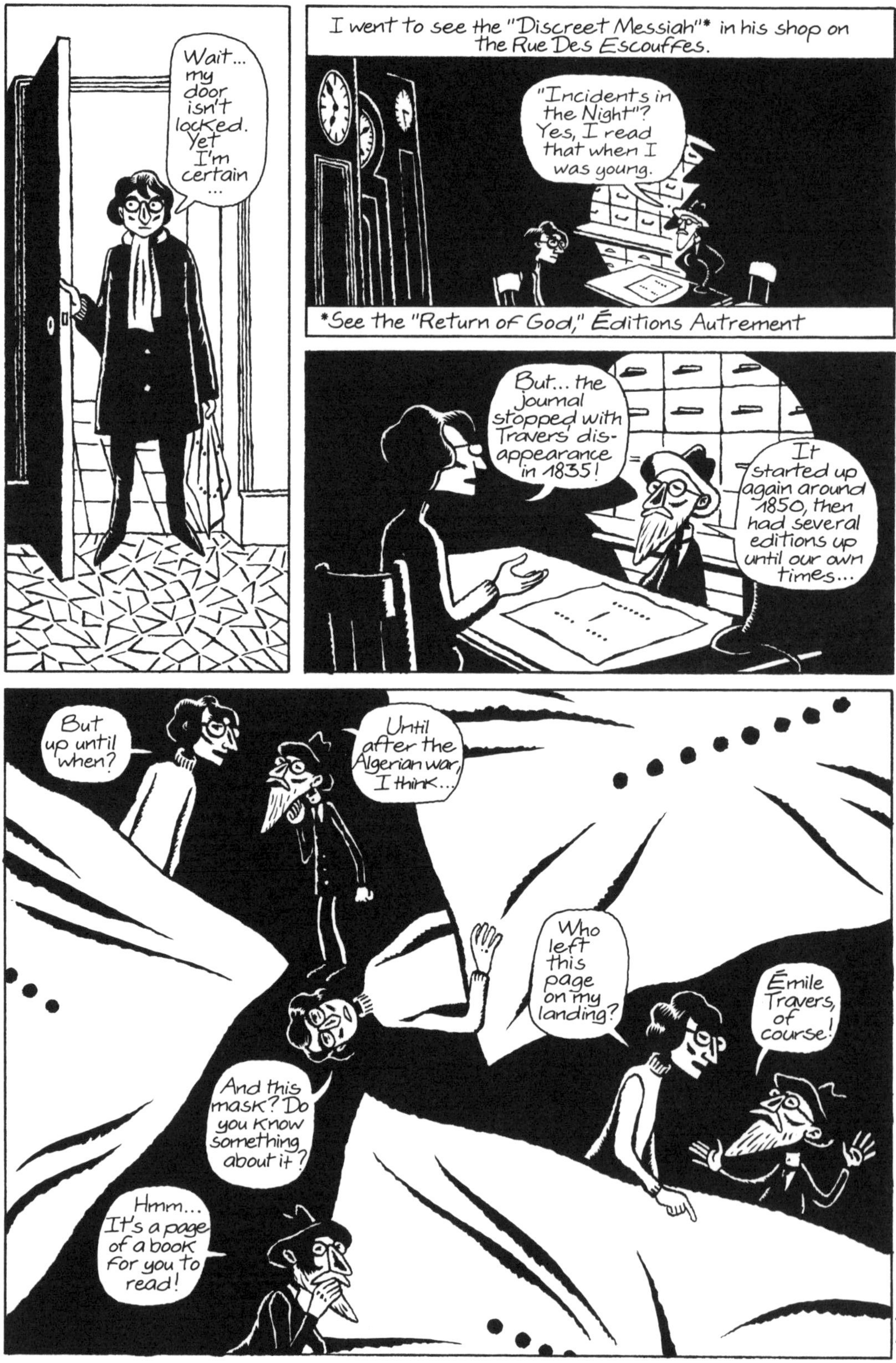

Wait... my door isn't locked. Yet I'm certain ...
I went to see the "Discreet Messiah"* in his shop on the Rue Des Escouffes.
"Incidents in the Night"? Yes, I read that when I was young.
*See the "Return of God," Éditions Autrement
But... the journal stopped with Travers' disappearance in 1835!
It started up again around 1850, then had several editions up until our own times...
But up until when?
Until after the Algerian war, I think...
Who left this page on my landing?
Émile Travers, of course!
And this mask? Do you know something about it?
Hmm... It's a page of a book for you to read!

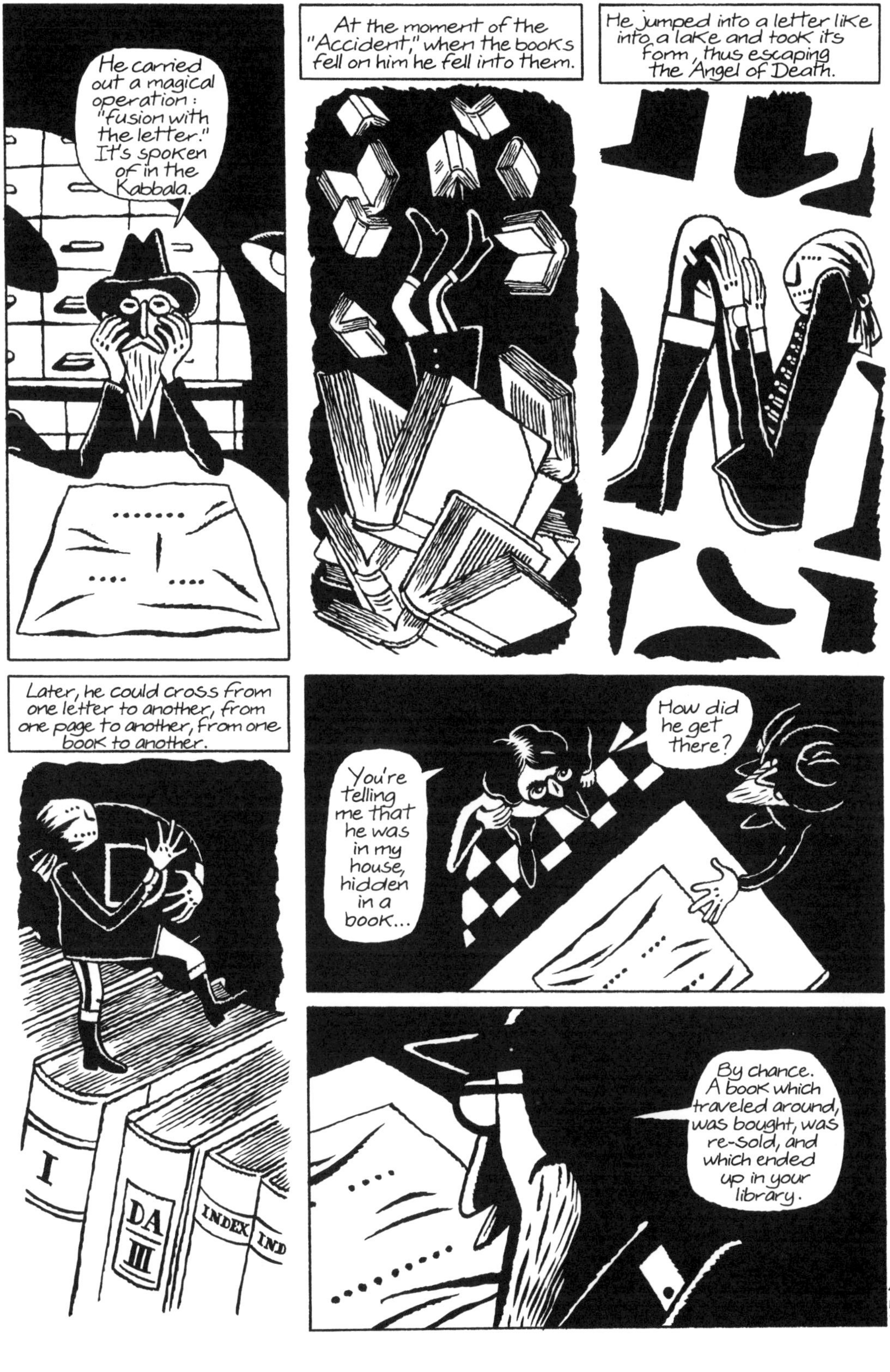
He carried out a magical operation: "fusion with the letter." It's spoken of in the Kabbala.
At the moment of the "Accident," when the books fell on him he fell into them.
He jumped into a letter like into a lake and took its form, thus escaping the Angel of Death.
Later, he could cross from one letter to another, from one page to another, from one book to another.
I
DA III
INDEX
IND
You're telling me that he was in my house, hidden in a book...
How did he get there?
By chance. A book which traveled around, was bought, was re-sold, and which ended up in your library.

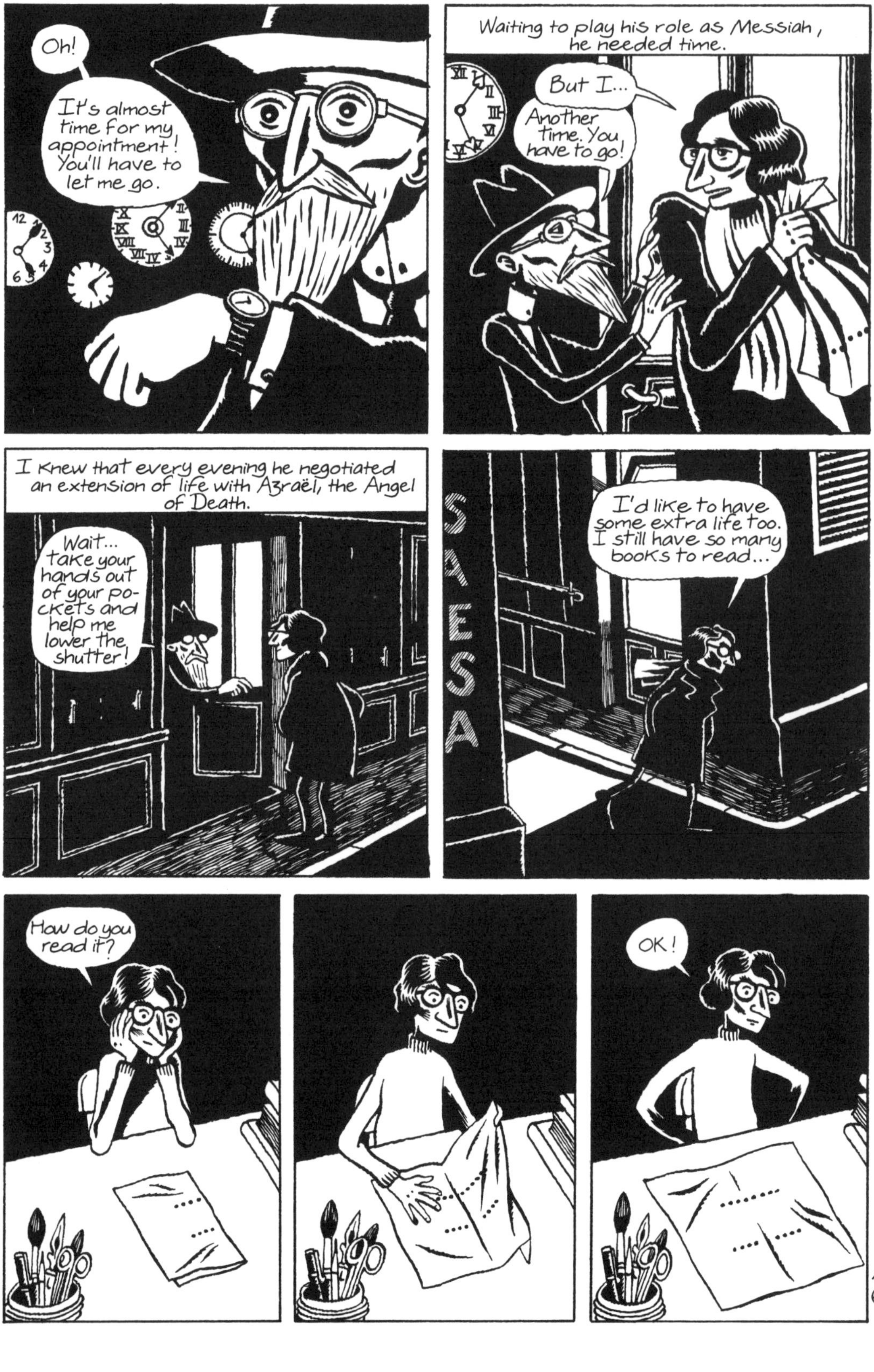
Oh!
It's almost time for my appointment! You'll have to let me go.
Waiting to play his role as Messiah, he needed time.
But I...
Another time. You have to go!
I knew that every evening he negotiated an extension of life with Azraël, the Angel of Death.
Wait... take your hands out of your pockets and help me lower the shutter!
SAESA
I'd like to have some extra life too. I still have so many books to read...
How do you read it?
OK!

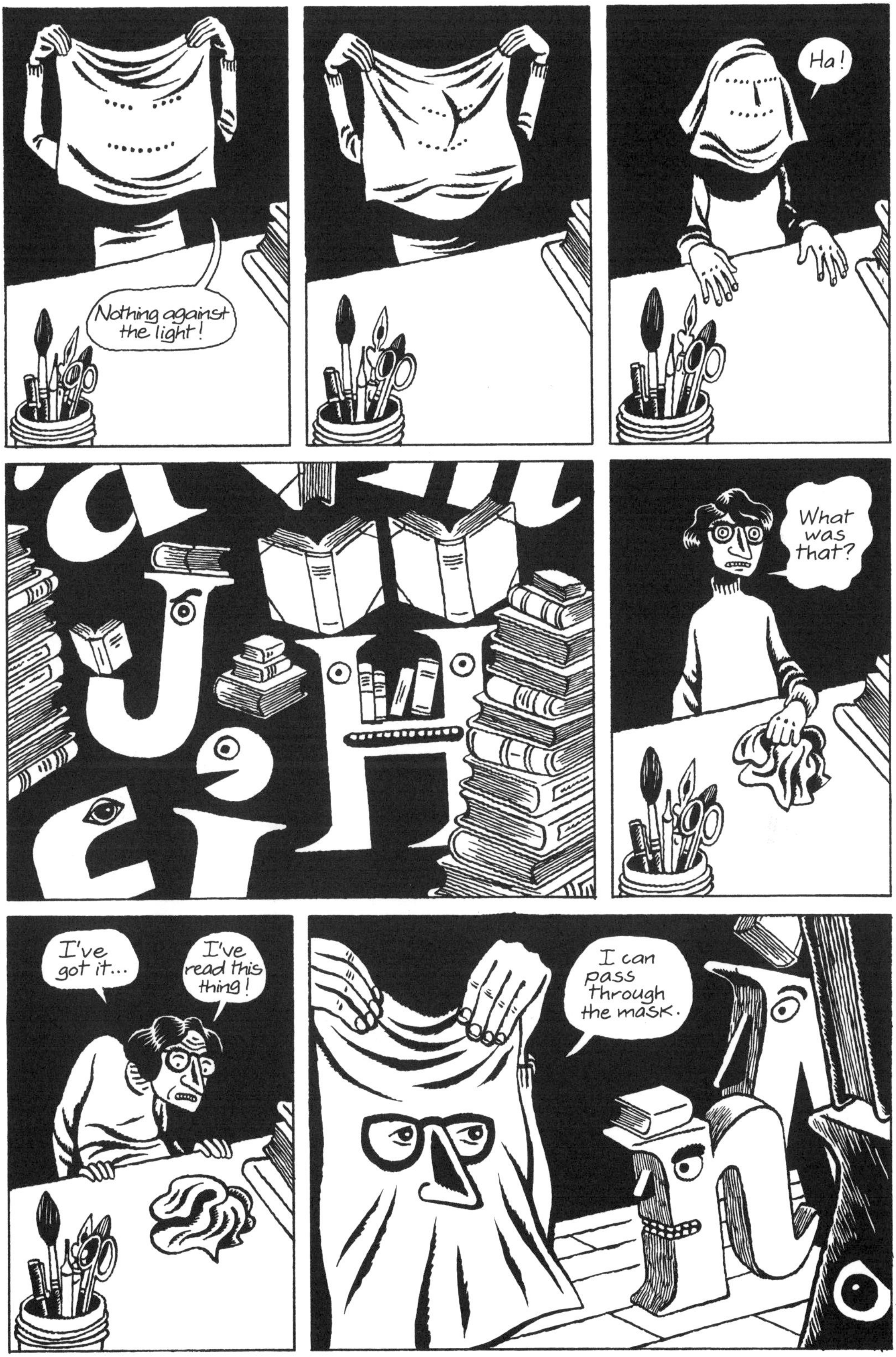
Nothing against the light!
Ha!
What was that?
I've got it...
I've read this thing!
I can pass through the mask.

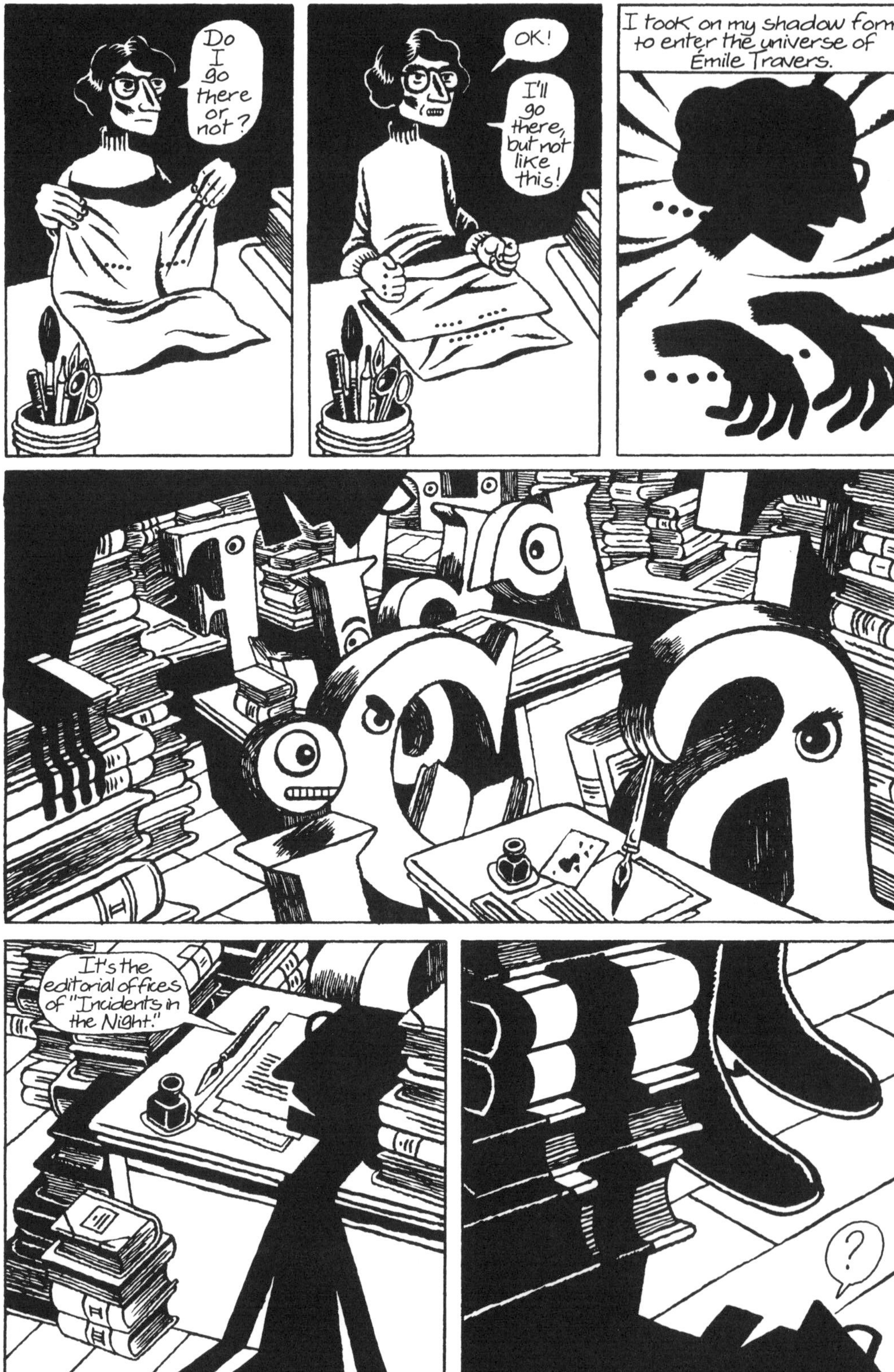
Do I go there or not?
OK!
I'll go there, but not like this!
I took on my shadow form to enter the universe of Émile Travers.
It's the editorial offices of "Incidents in the Night."
?

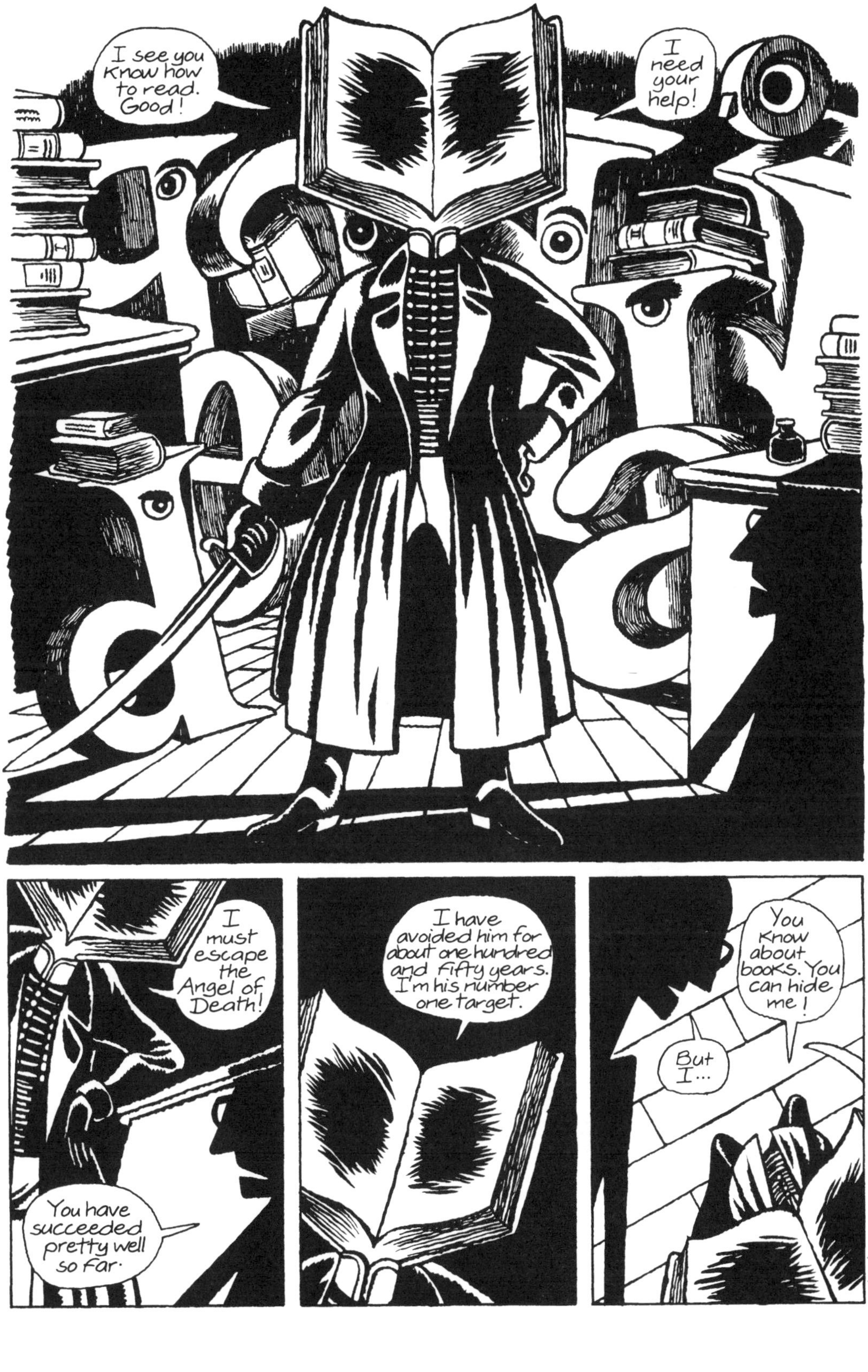

I see you know how to read. Good!
I need your help!
I must escape the Angel of Death!
You have succeeded pretty well so far.
I have avoided him for about one hundred and fifty years. I'm his number one target.
You know about books. You can hide me!
But I...

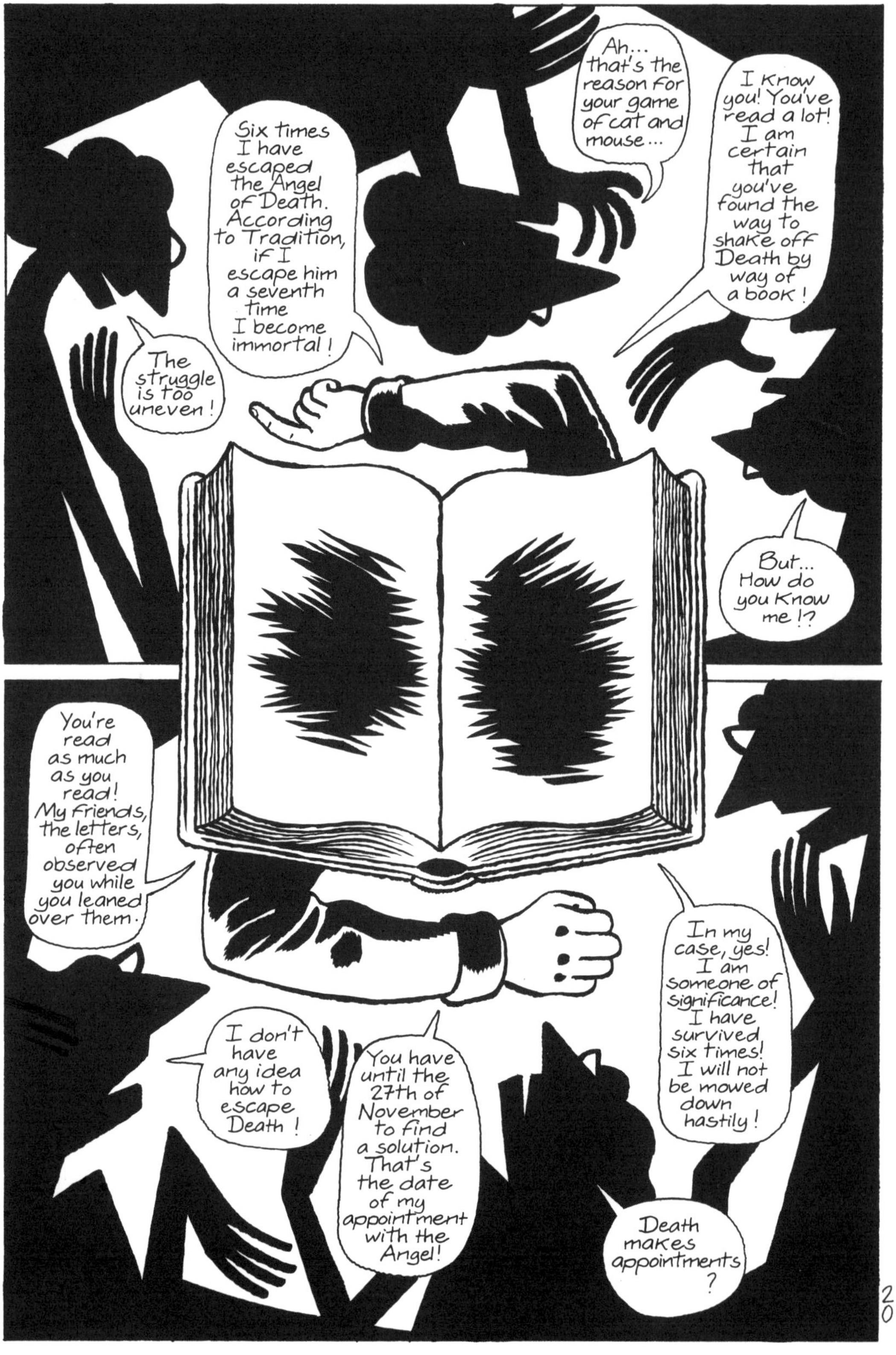
Six times I have escaped the Angel of Death. According to Tradition, if I escape him a seventh time I become immortal!
The struggle is too uneven!
Ah... that's the reason for your game of cat and mouse...
I know you! You've read a lot! I am certain that you've found the way to shake off Death by way of a book!
But... How do you know me!?
You're read as much as you read! My friends, the letters, often observed you while you leaned over them.
In my case, yes! I am someone of significance! I have survived six times! I will not be mowed down hastily!
I don't have any idea how to escape Death!
You have until the 27th of November to find a solution. That's the date of my appointment with the Angel!
Death makes appointments?

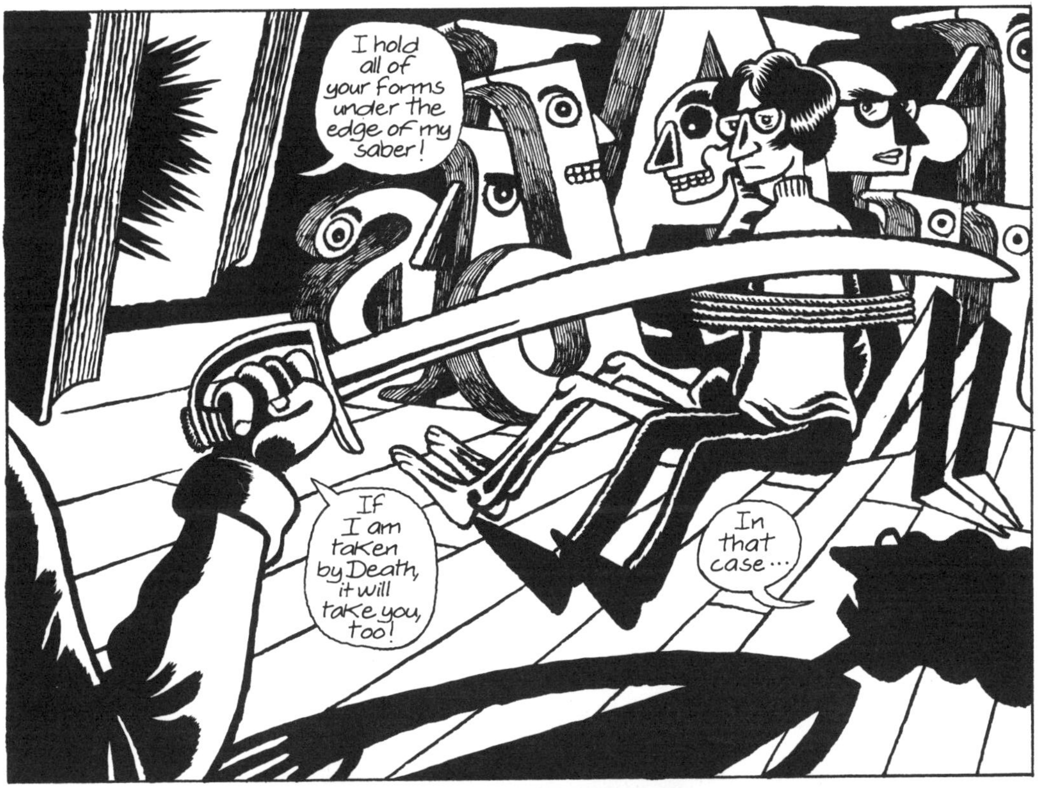
I hold all of your forms under the edge of my saber!
If I am taken by Death, it will take you, too!
In that case...

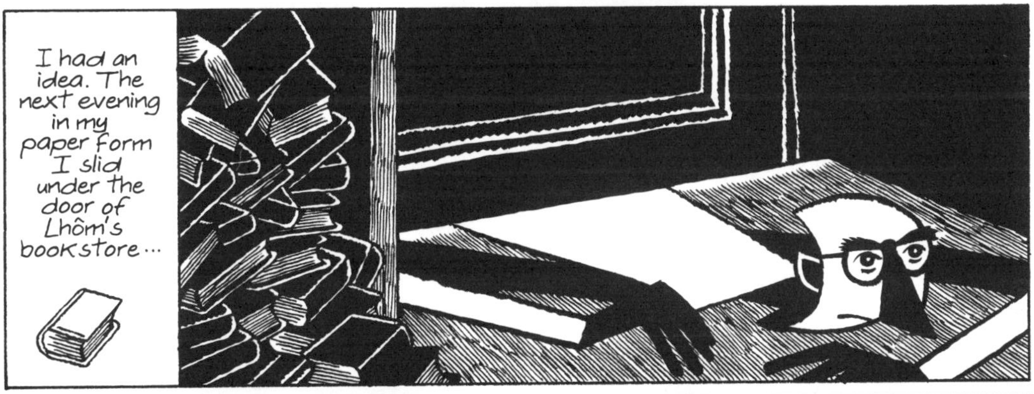
I had an idea. The next evening in my paper form I slid under the door of Lhôm's bookstore...

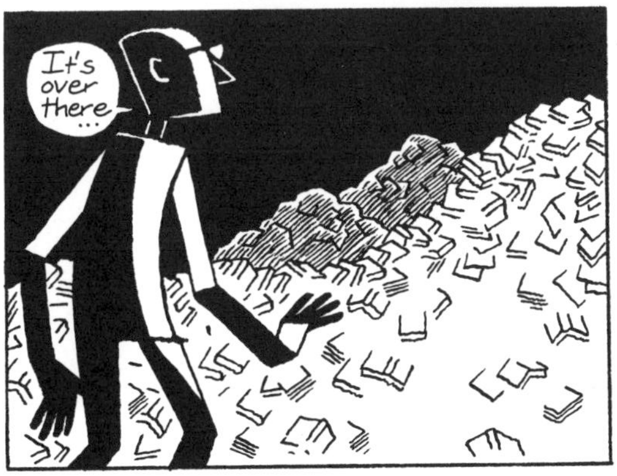
It's over there...

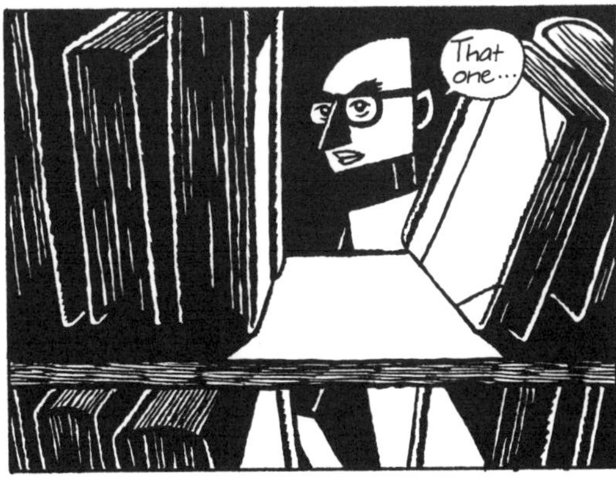
That one...

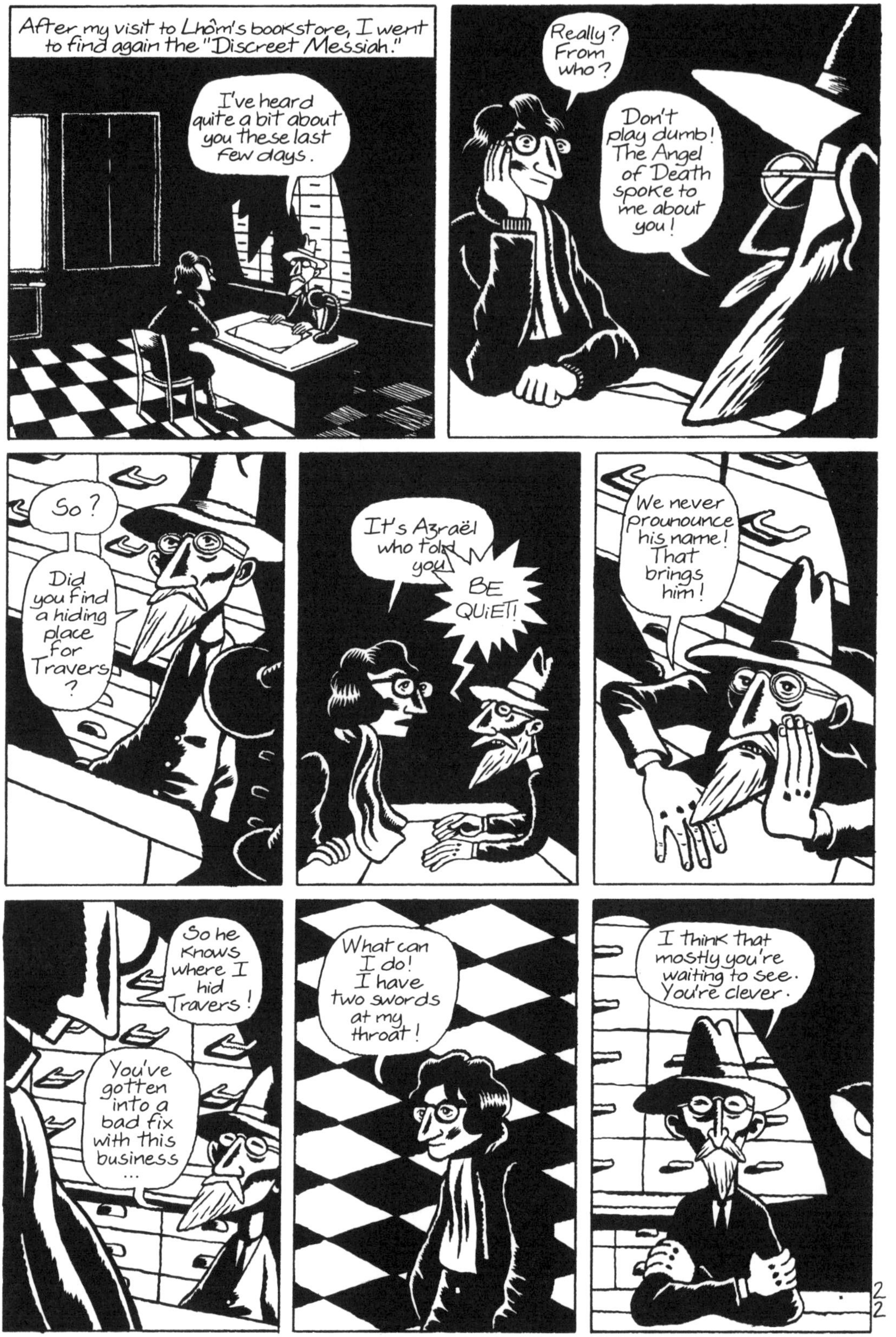
After my visit to Lhôm's bookstore, I went to find again the "Discreet Messiah."
I've heard quite a bit about you these last few days.
Really? From who?
Don't play dumb! The Angel of Death spoke to me about you!
So?
Did you find a hiding place for Travers?
It's Azraël who told you
BE QUIET!
We never prounounce his name! That brings him!
So he knows where I hid Travers!
You've gotten into a bad fix with this business...
What can I do! I have two swords at my throat!
I think that mostly you're waiting to see. You're clever.

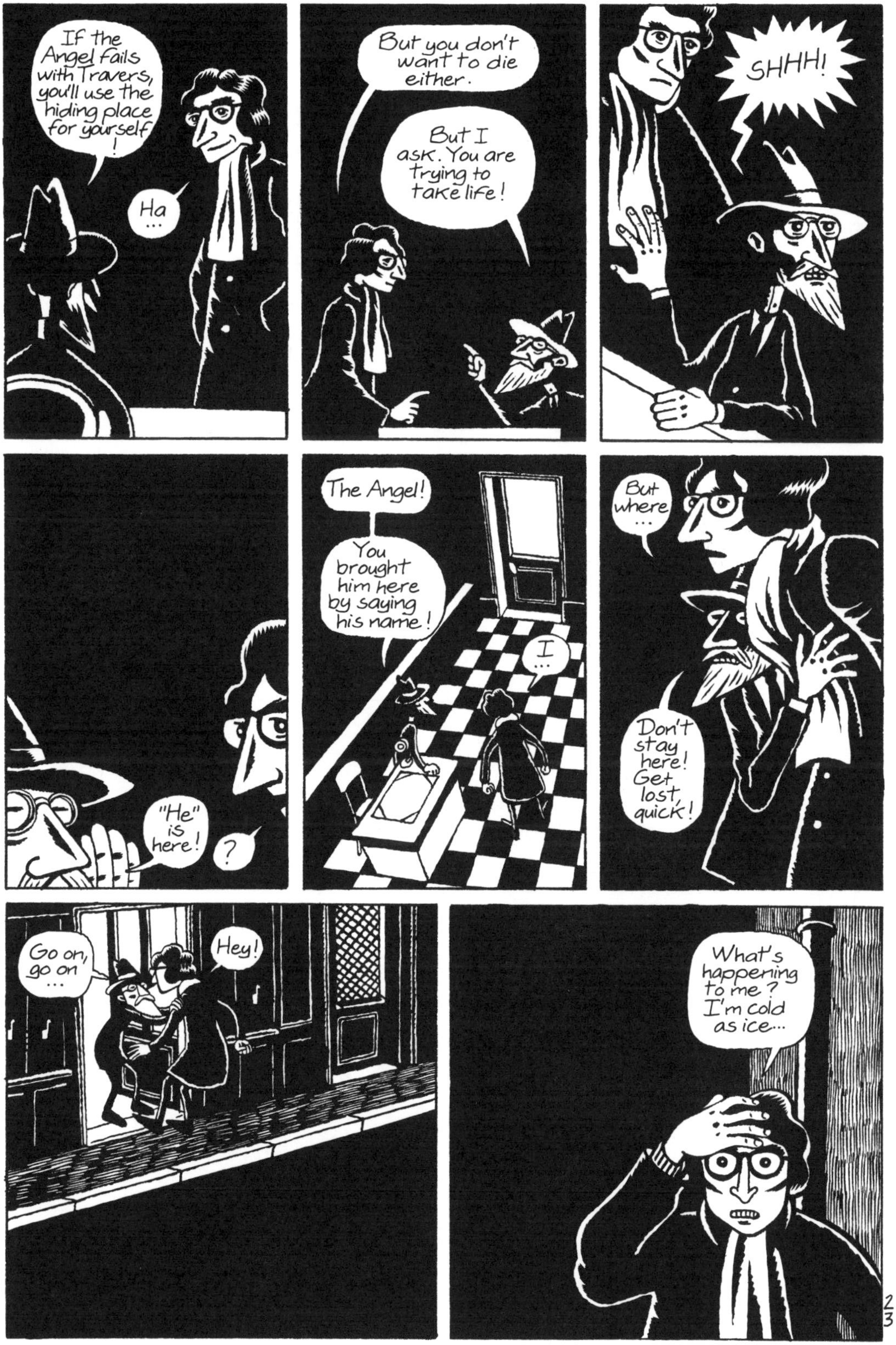
If the Angel fails with Travers, you'll use the hiding place for yourself!
Ha...
But you don't want to die either.
But I ask. You are trying to take life!
SHHH!
"He" is here!
?
The Angel!
You brought him here by saying his name!
I...
But where...
Don't stay here! Get lost, quick!
Go on, go on...
Hey!
What's happening to me? I'm cold as ice...

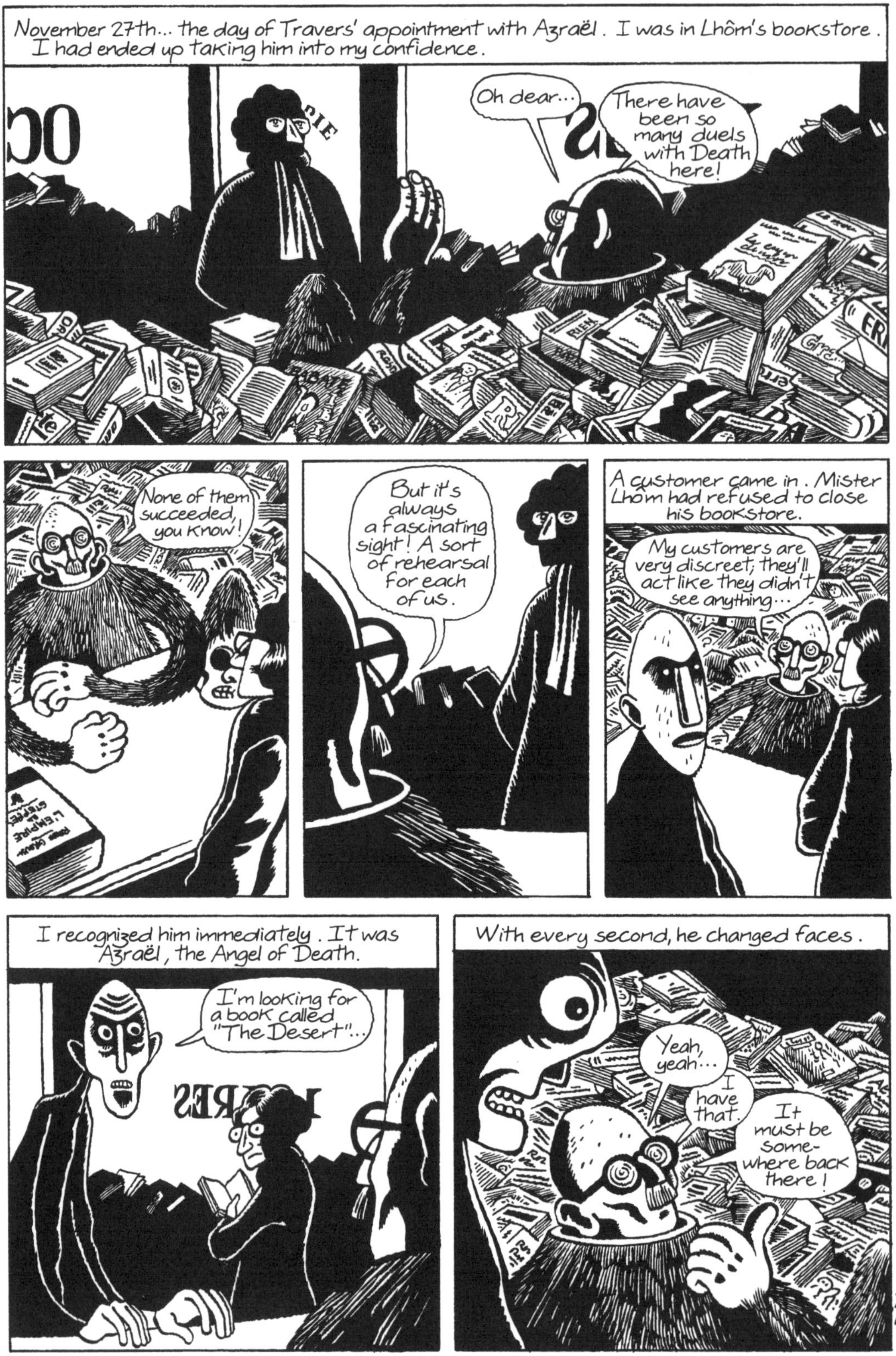
November 27th... the day of Travers' appointment with Azraël. I was in Lhôm's bookstore. I had ended up taking him into my confidence.
Oh dear...
There have been so many duels with Death here!
None of them succeeded, you know!
But it's always a fascinating sight! A sort of rehearsal for each of us.
A customer came in. Mister Lhôm had refused to close his bookstore.
My customers are very discreet; they'll act like they didn't see anything...
I recognized him immediately. It was Azraël, the Angel of Death.
I'm looking for a book called "The Desert"...
With every second, he changed faces.
Yeah, yeah...
I have that.
It must be some-where back there!

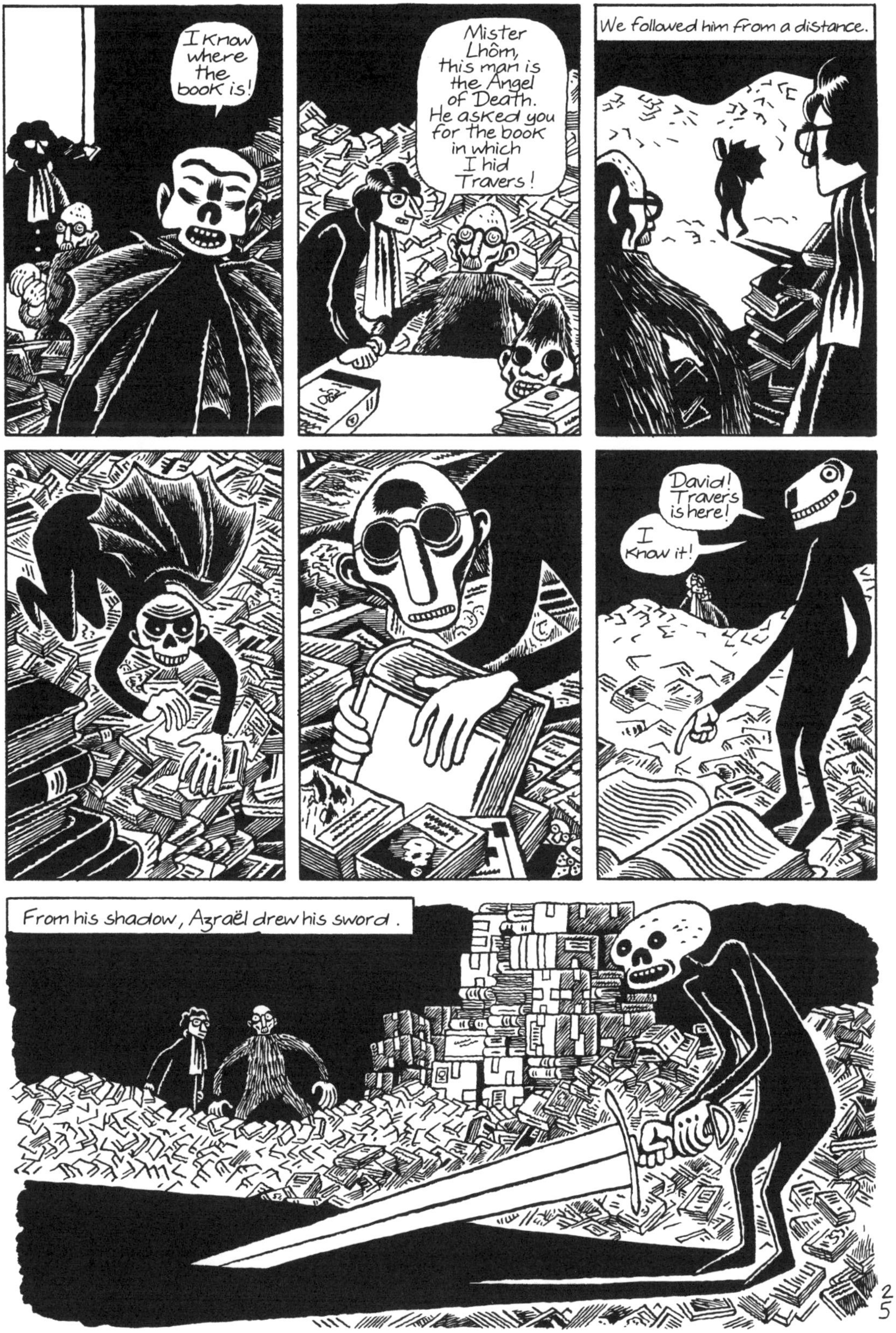
I know where the book is!
Mister Lhôm, this man is the Angel of Death. He asked you for the book in which I hid Travers!
We followed him from a distance.
David! Travers is here!
I know it!
From his shadow, Azraël drew his sword.

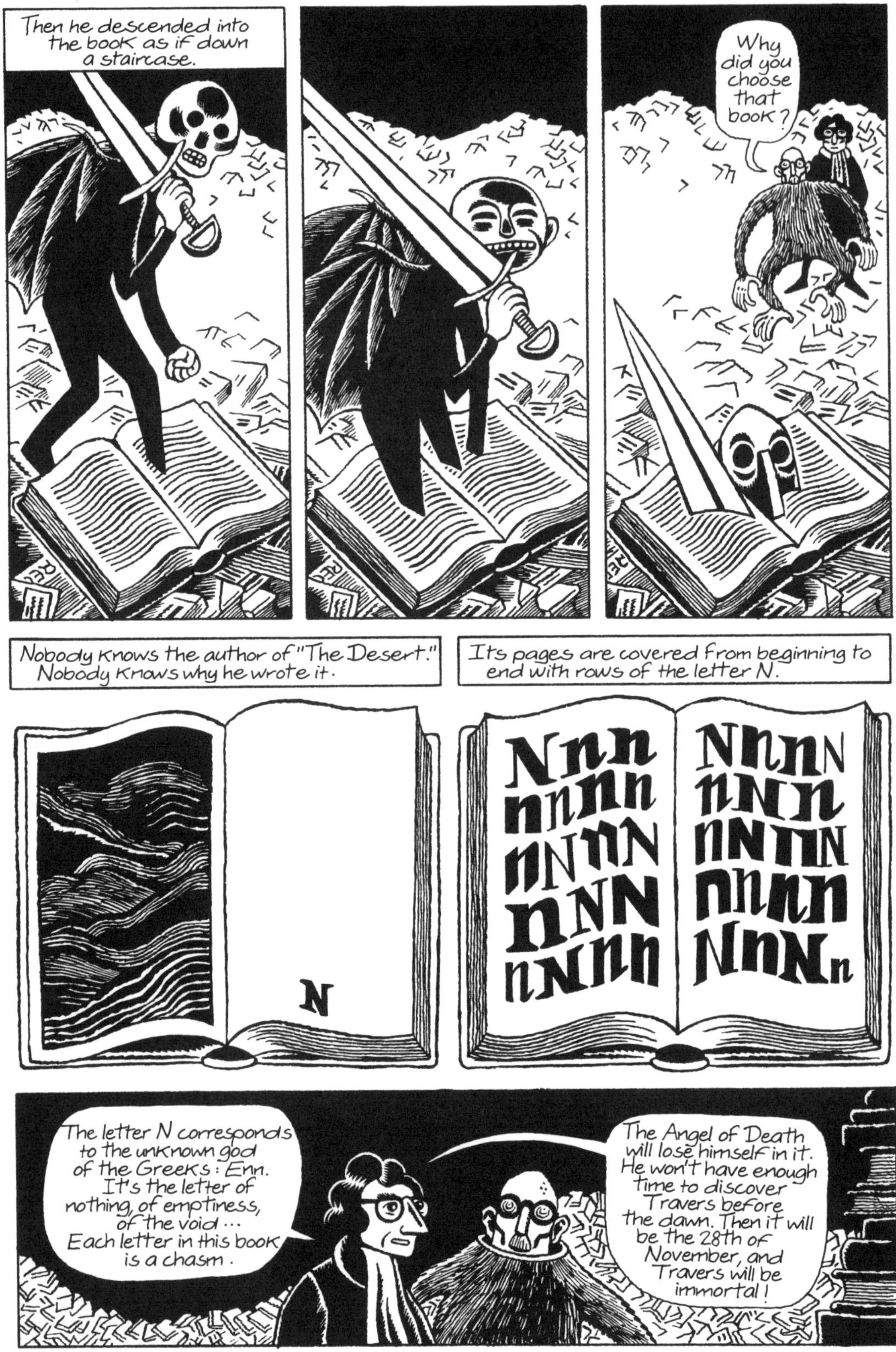
Then he descended into the book as if down a staircase.
Why did you choose that book?
Nobody knows the author of "The Desert." Nobody knows why he wrote it.
Its pages are covered from beginning to end with rows of the letter N.
The letter N corresponds to the unknown god of the Greeks: Enn. It's the letter of nothing, of emptiness, of the void... Each letter in this book is a chasm.
The Angel of Death will lose himself in it. He won't have enough time to discover Travers before the dawn. Then it will be the 28th of November, and Travers will be immortal!

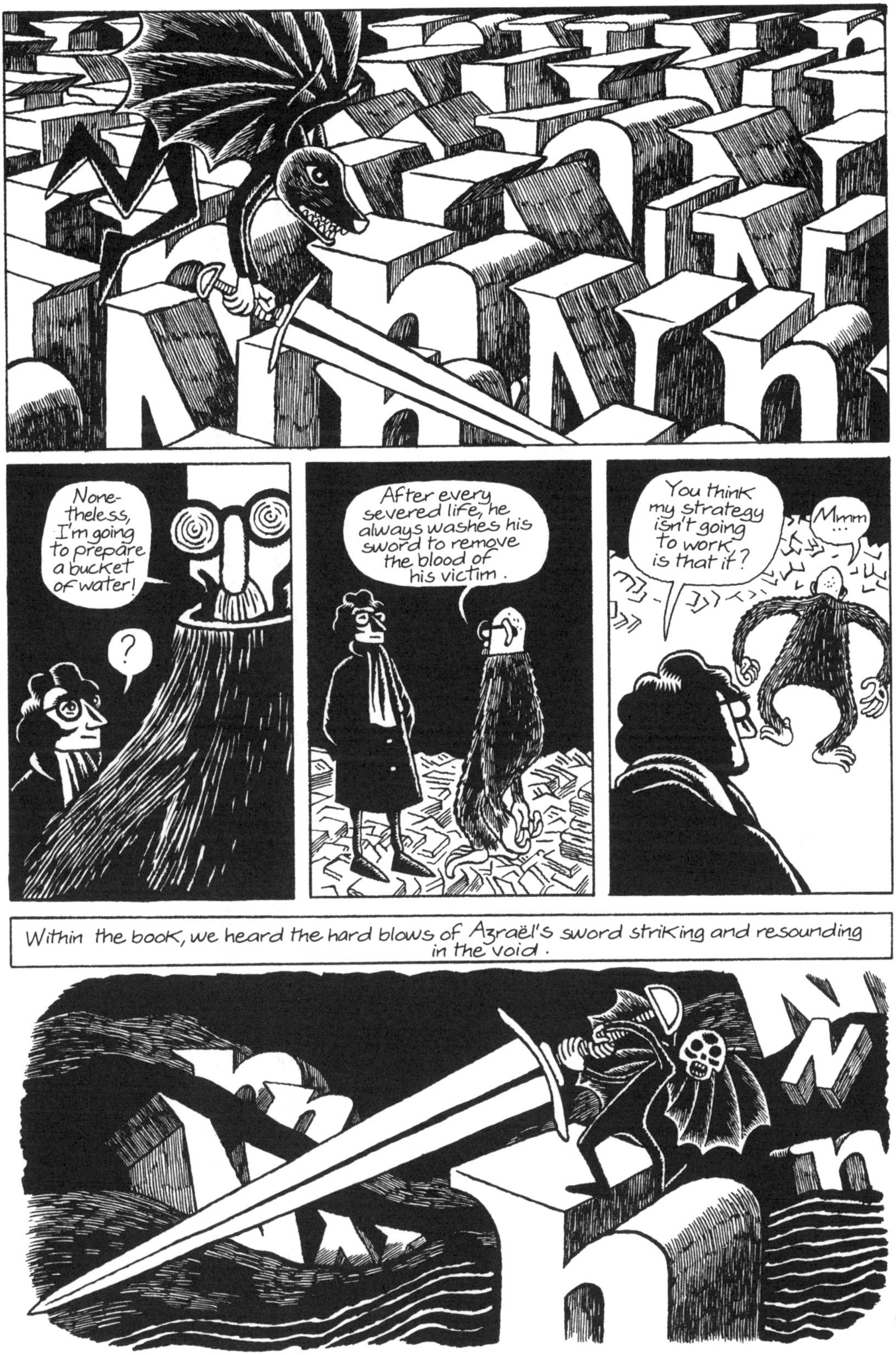
None-theless, I'm going to prepare a bucket of water!
?
After every severed life, he always washes his sword to remove the blood of his victim.
You think my strategy isn't going to work, is that it?
Mmm...
Within the book, we heard the hard blows of Azraël's sword striking and resounding in the void.

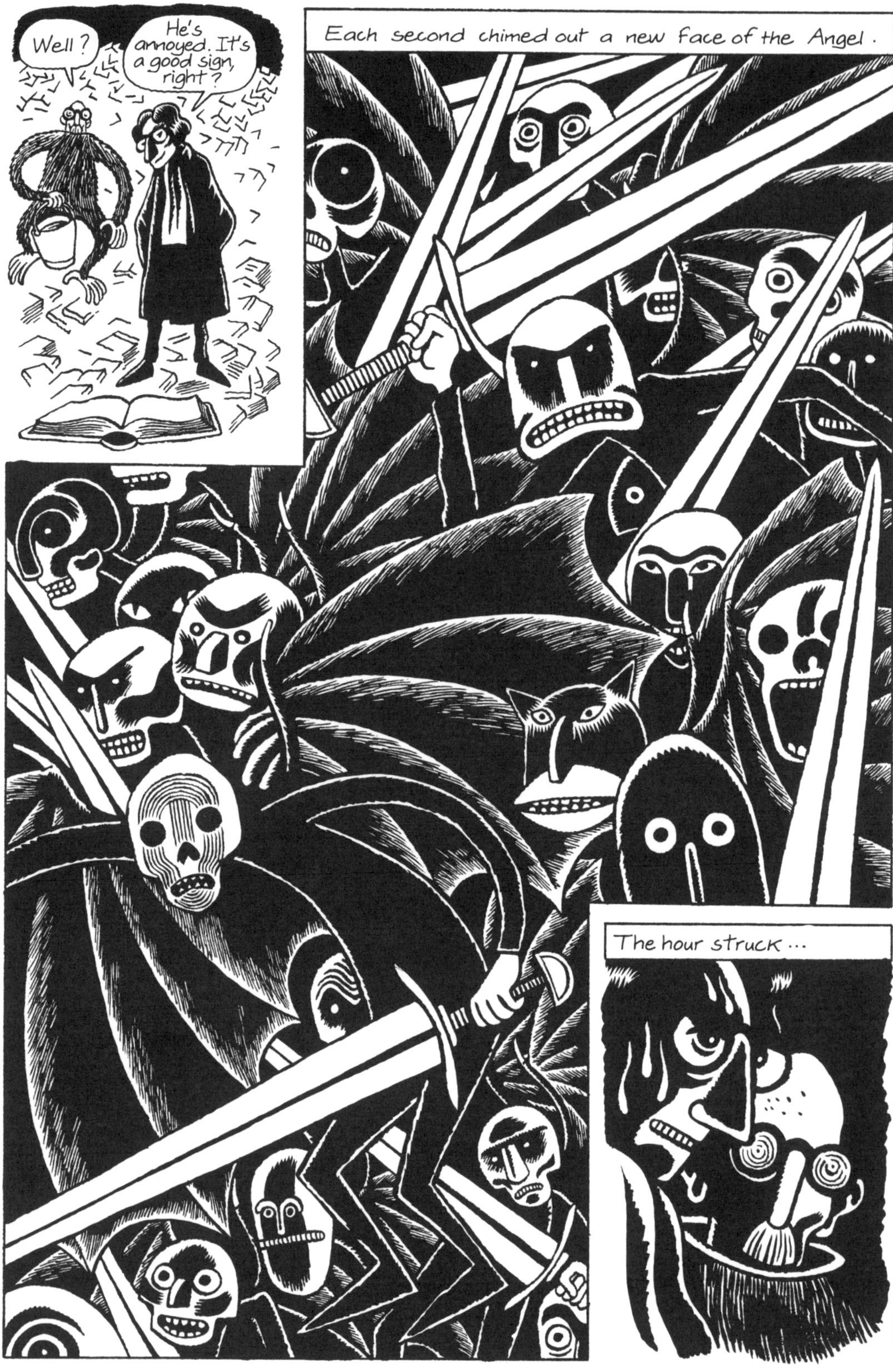
Well?
He's annoyed. It's a good sign, right?
Each second chimed out a new face of the Angel.
The hour struck ...

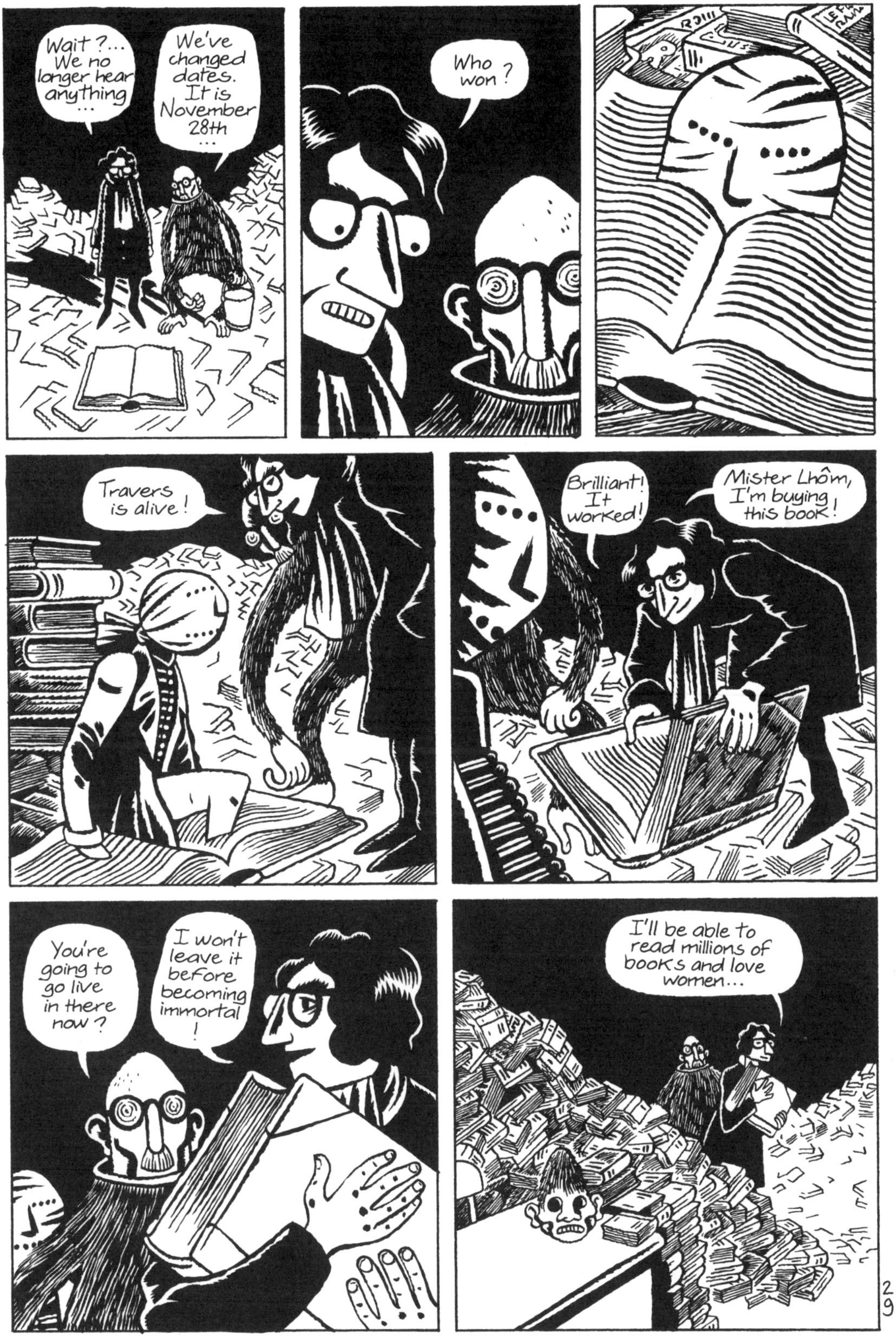
Wait?... We no longer hear anything ...
We've changed dates. It is November 28th ...
Who won?
Travers is alive!
Brilliant! It worked!
Mister Lhôm, I'm buying this book!
You're going to go live in there now?
I won't leave it before becoming immortal!
I'll be able to read millions of books and love women...

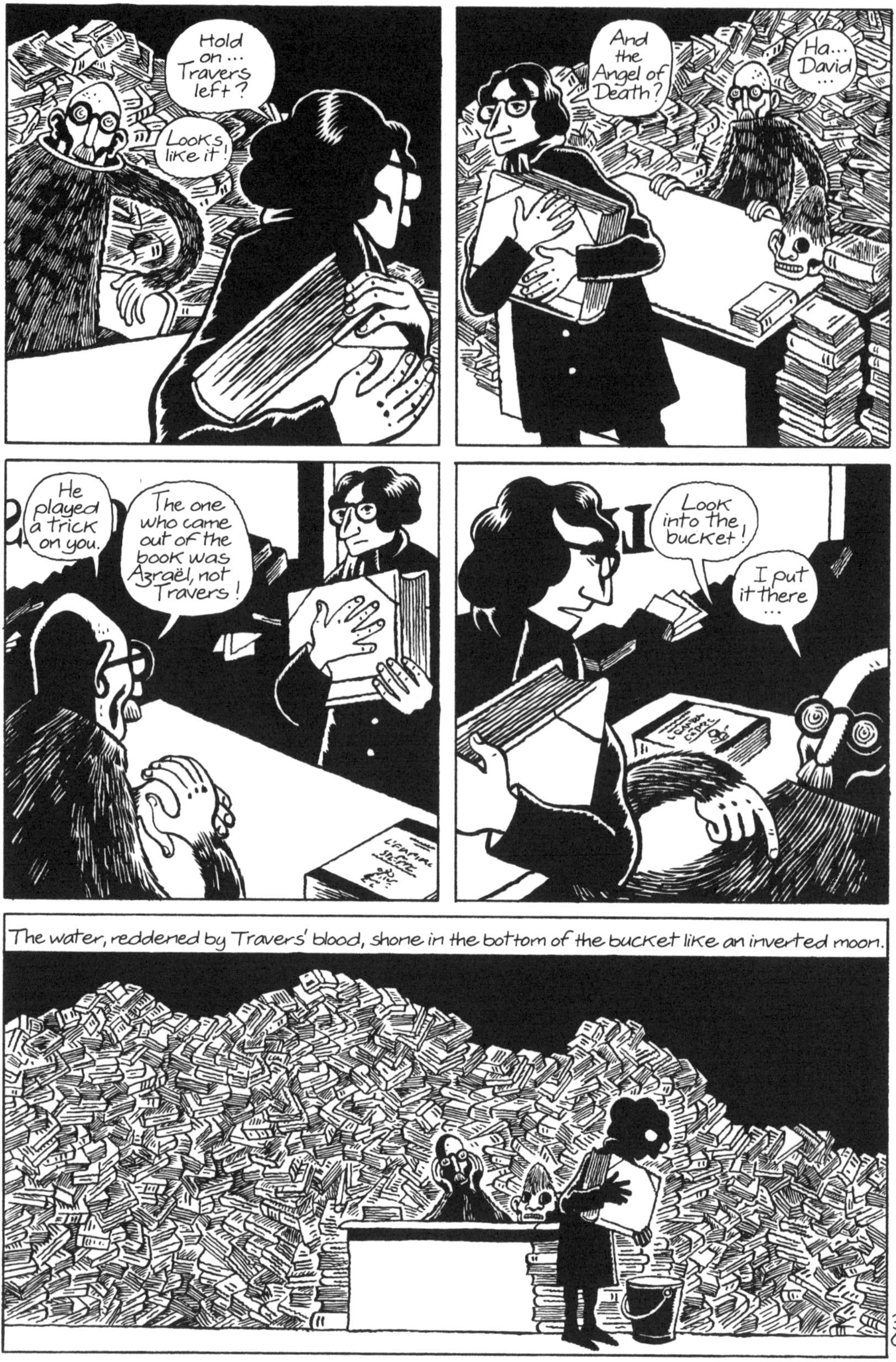
Hold on ... Travers left?
Looks like it!
And the Angel of Death?
Ha... David ...
He played a trick on you.
The one who came out of the book was Azraël, not Travers!
Look into the bucket!
I put it there ...
The water, reddened by Travers' blood, shone in the bottom of the bucket like an inverted moon.

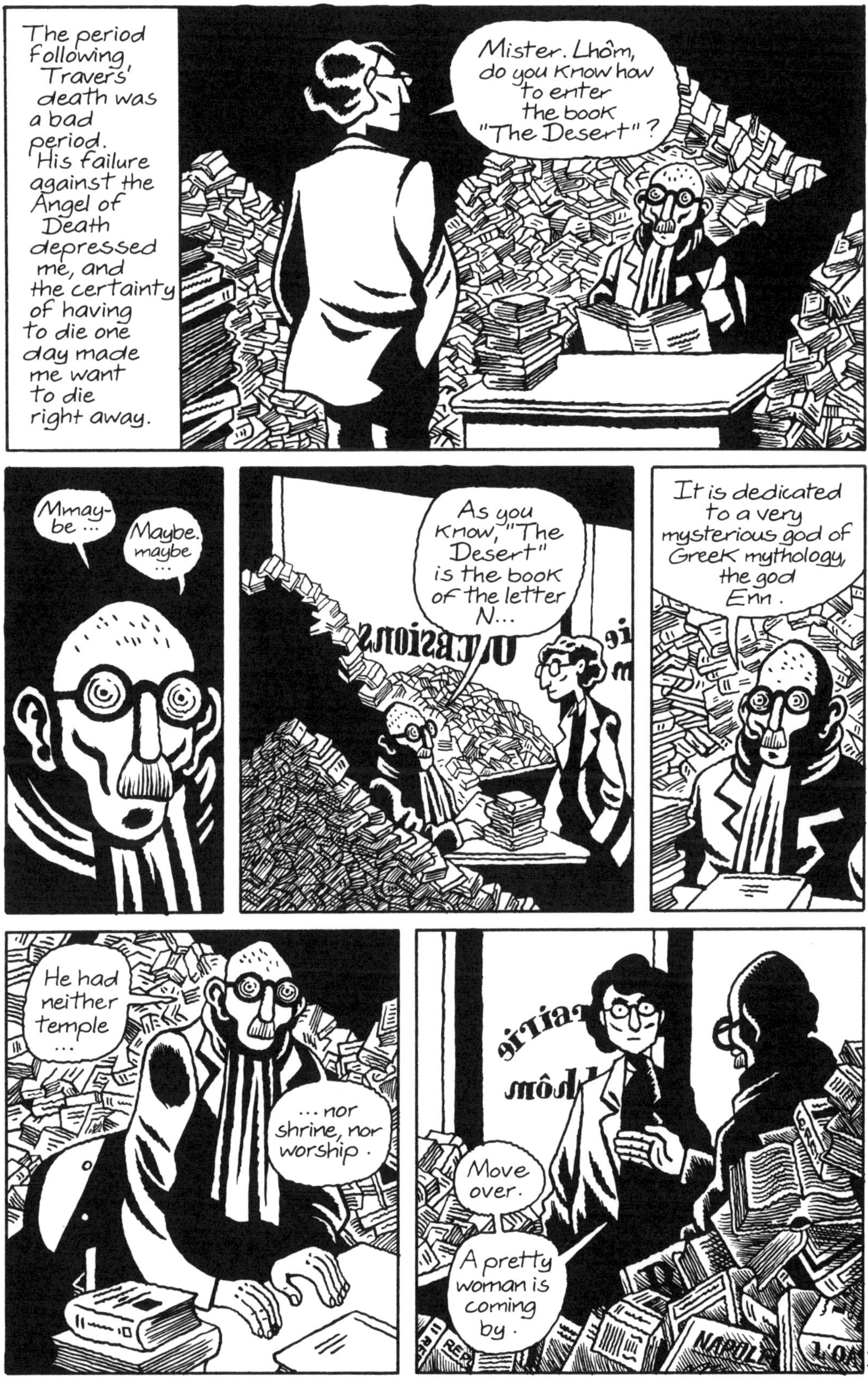
The period following Travers' death was a bad period. His failure against the Angel of Death depressed me, and the certainty of having to die one day made me want to die right away.
Mister. Lhôm, do you know how to enter the book "The Desert"?
Mmaybe...
Maybe. maybe...
As you know, "The Desert" is the book of the letter N...
It is dedicated to a very mysterious god of Greek mythology, the god Enn.
He had neither temple...
...nor shrine, nor worship.
Move over.
A pretty woman is coming by.

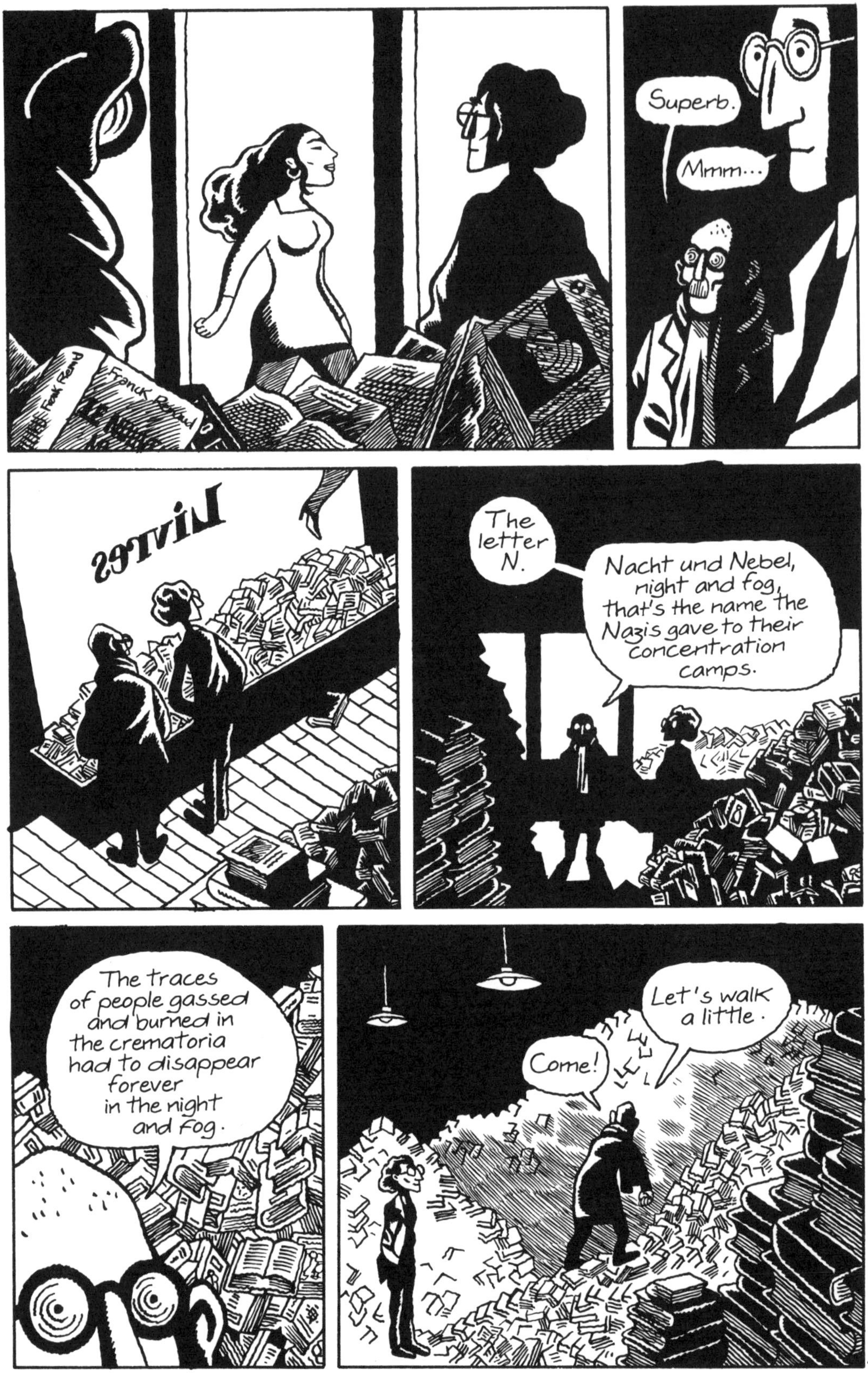
Superb.
Mmm...
The letter N.
Nacht und Nebel, night and fog, that's the name the Nazis gave to their concentration camps.
The traces of people gassed and burned in the crematoria had to disappear forever in the night and fog.
Come!
Let's walk a little.

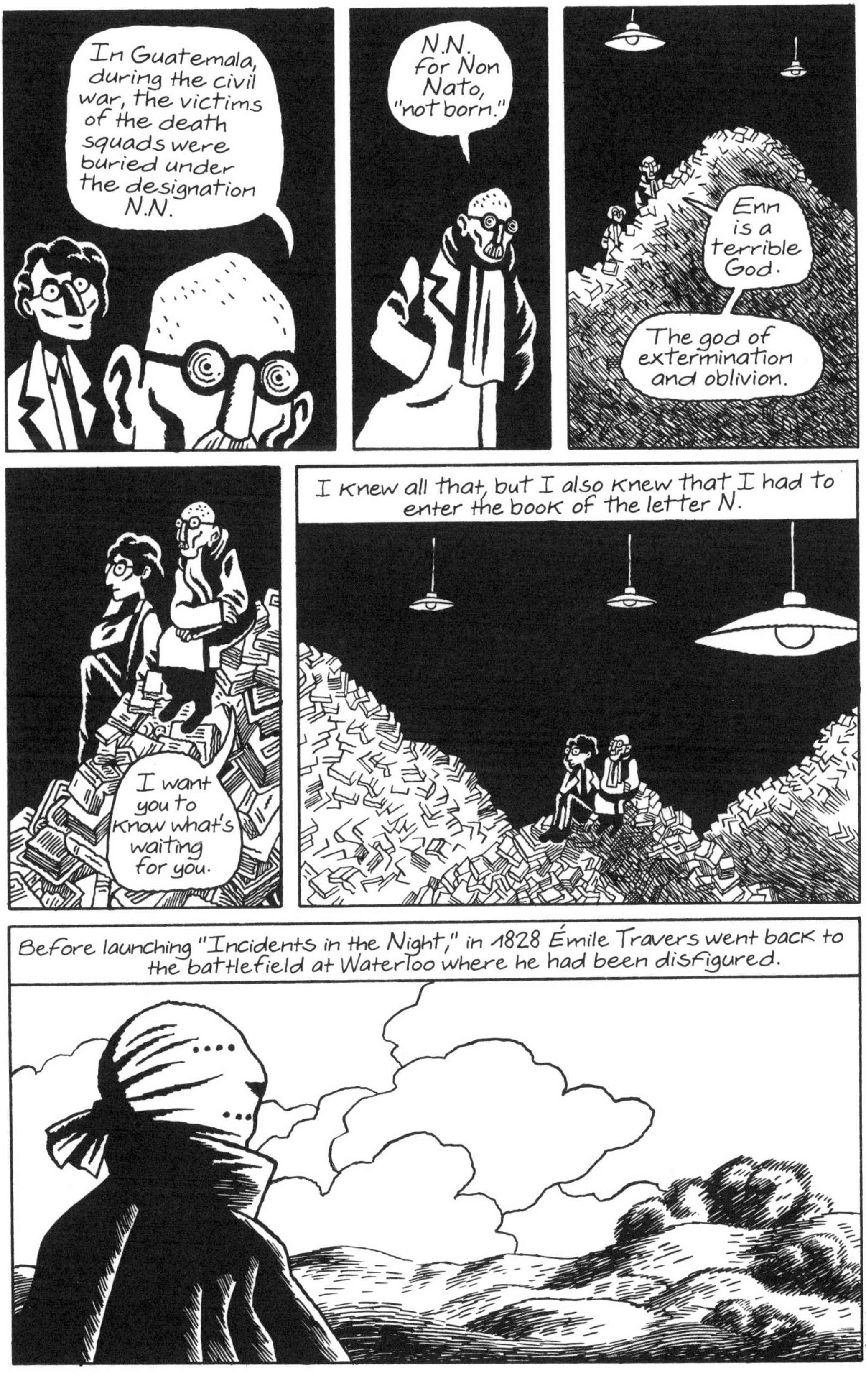
In Guatemala, during the civil war, the victims of the death squads were buried under the designation N.N.
N.N. for Non Nato, "not born."
Enn is a terrible God.
The god of extermination and oblivion.
I want you to know what's waiting for you.
I knew all that, but I also knew that I had to enter the book of the letter N.
Before launching "Incidents in the Night," in 1828 Émile Travers went back to the battlefield at Waterloo where he had been disfigured.

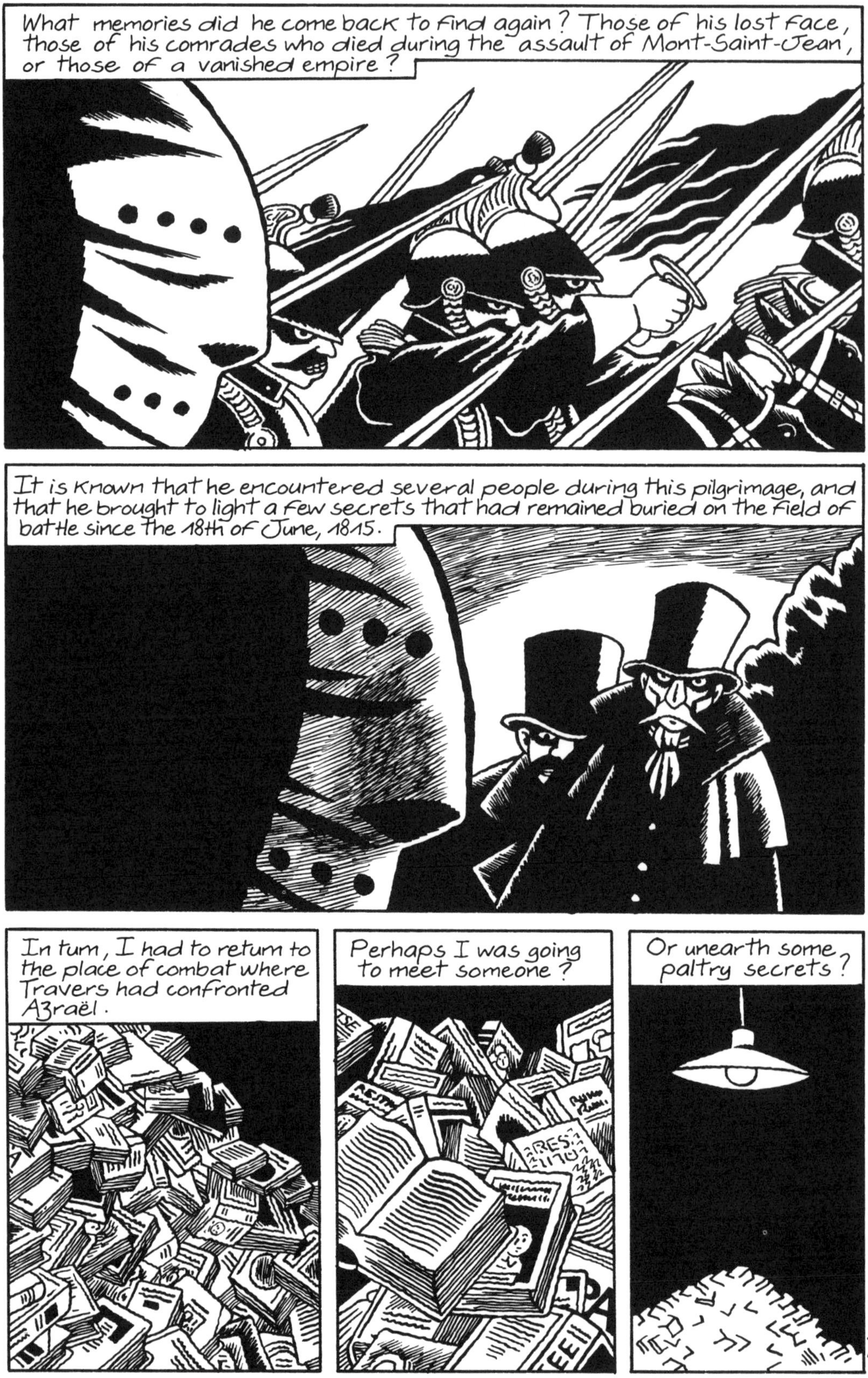
What memories did he come back to find again? Those of his lost face, those of his comrades who died during the assault of Mont-Saint-Jean, or those of a vanished empire?
It is known that he encountered several people during this pilgrimage, and that he brought to light a few secrets that had remained buried on the field of battle since the 18th of June, 1815.
In turn, I had to return to the place of combat where Travers had confronted Azraël.
Perhaps I was going to meet someone?
Or unearth some paltry secrets?

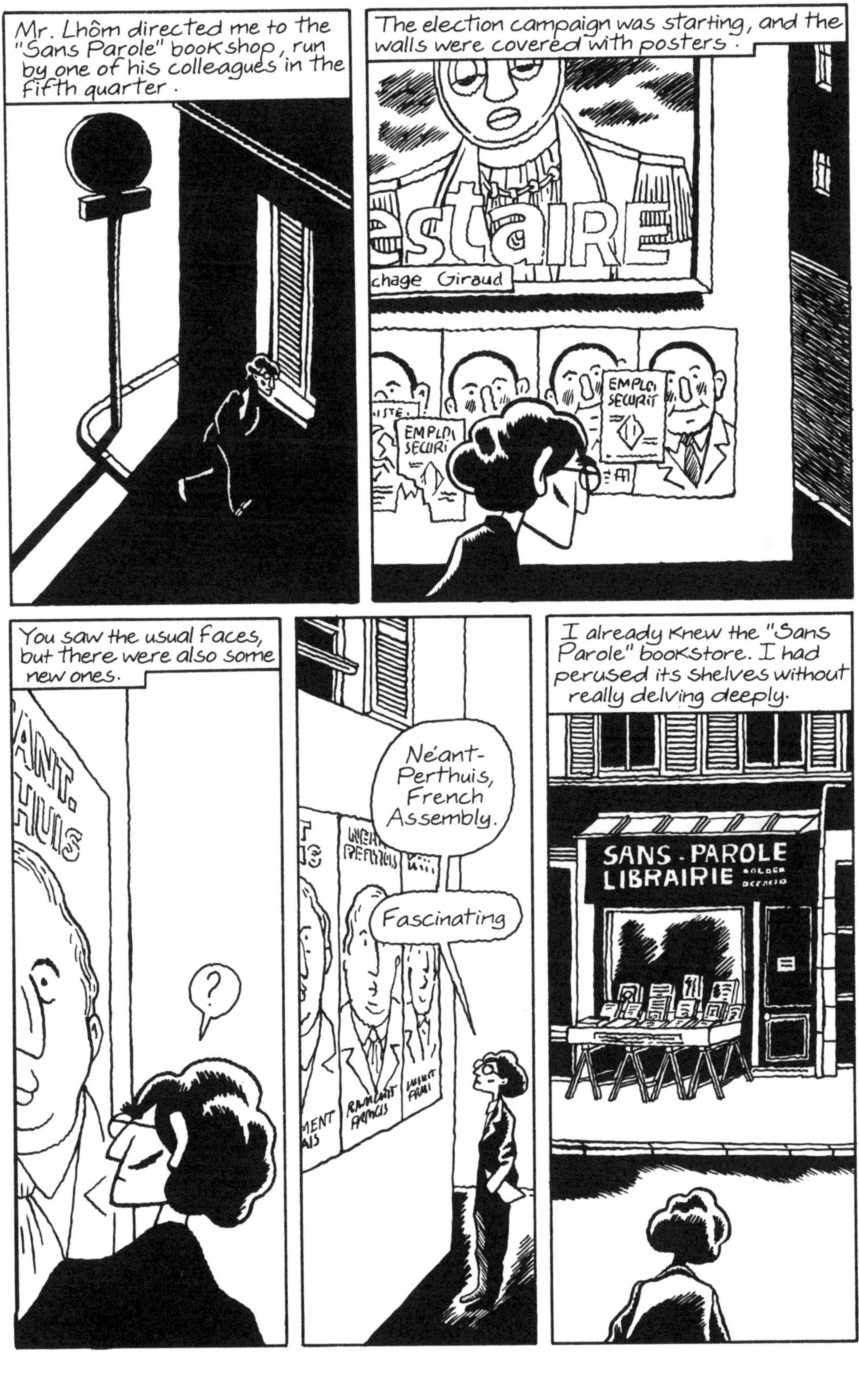
Mr. Lhôm directed me to the "Sans Parole" bookshop, run by one of his colleagues in the fifth quarter.
The election campaign was starting, and the walls were covered with posters.
chage Giraud
You saw the usual faces, but there were also some new ones.
?
Néant-Perthuis, French Assembly.
Fascinating
I already knew the "Sans Parole" bookstore. I had perused its shelves without really delving deeply.
SANS-PAROLE
LIBRAIRIE

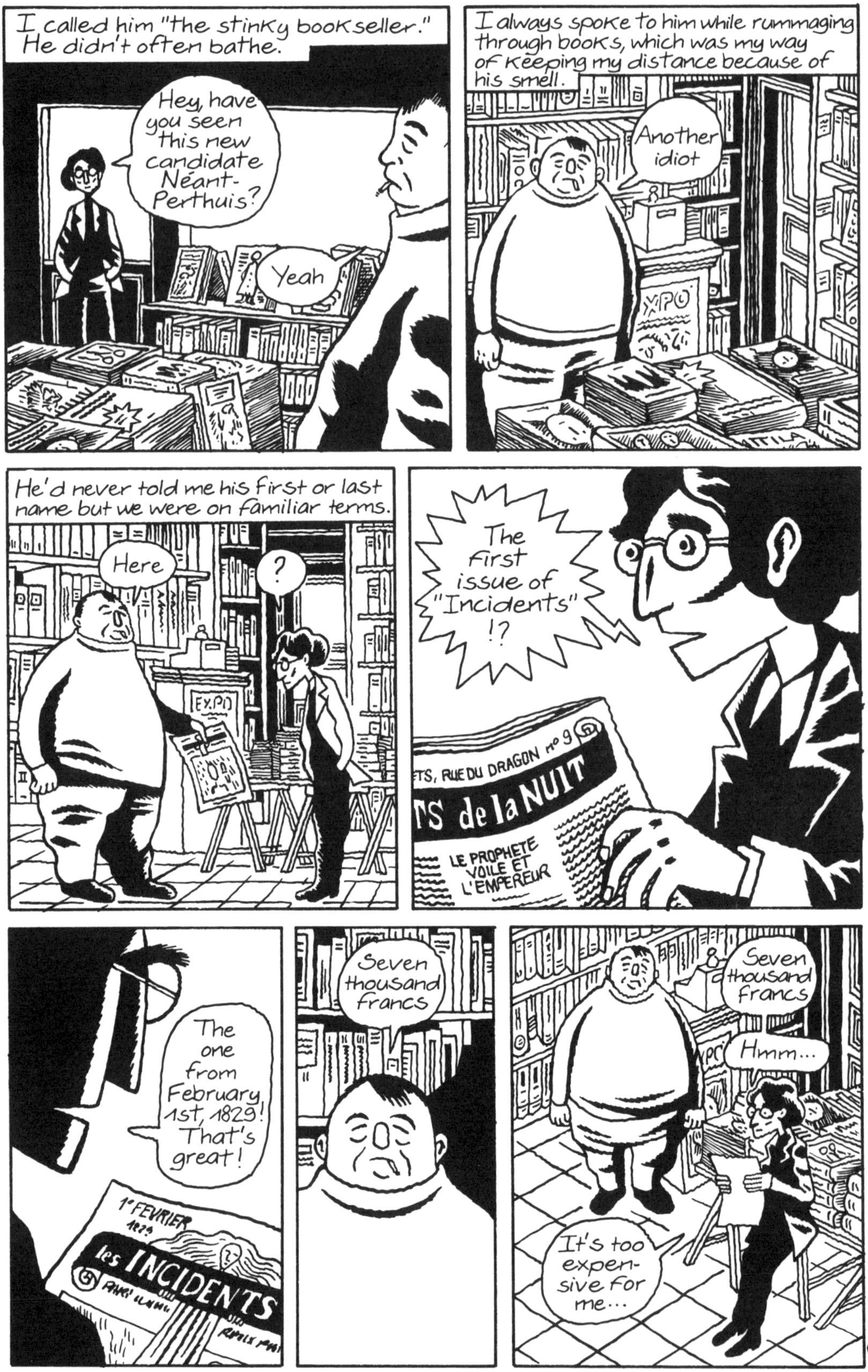
I called him "the stinky bookseller." He didn't often bathe.
Hey, have you seen this new candidate Néant-Perthuis?
Yeah
I always spoke to him while rummaging through books, which was my way of keeping my distance because of his smell.
Another idiot
He'd never told me his first or last name but we were on familiar terms.
Here
?
EXPO
The first issue of "Incidents" !?
TS, RUE DU DRAGON No 9
TS de la NUIT
LE PROPHETE VOILE ET L'EMPEREUR
The one from February 1st, 1829! That's great!
1er FEVRIER 1829
les INCIDENTS
Seven thousand francs
Seven thousand francs
Hmm...
It's too expensive for me...

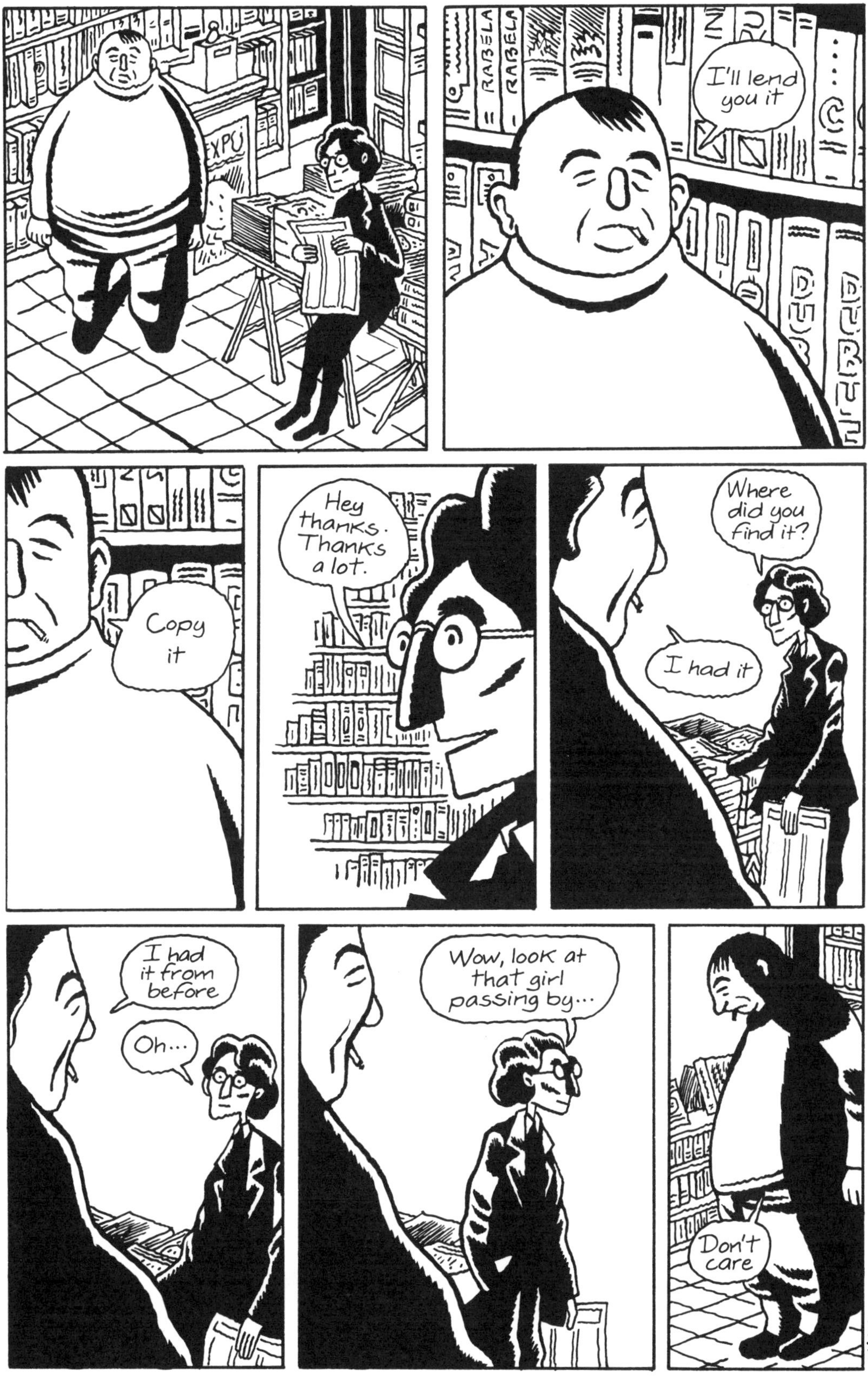
I'll lend you it
Copy it
Hey thanks. Thanks a lot.
Where did you find it?
I had it
I had it from before
Oh...
Wow, look at that girl passing by...
Don't care

Oh
...

I'm off
thanks again
for the
journal.

'bye

The stinky bookseller didn't like anything
that reminded him of "before."

SANS PAROLE
LIBRAIRIE
SOLDES OCCASIONS

Before he had landed in a bookshop
that was full of old books that were
as grubby as he.

M

"Incidents
in the Night"
was four
pages long.
First, there
was a
long article
on the
betrayal by
the captain
of the
carabiniers,
Barail,
during the
battle
of
Waterloo.

LONG
LIVE THE
KING!

3
8

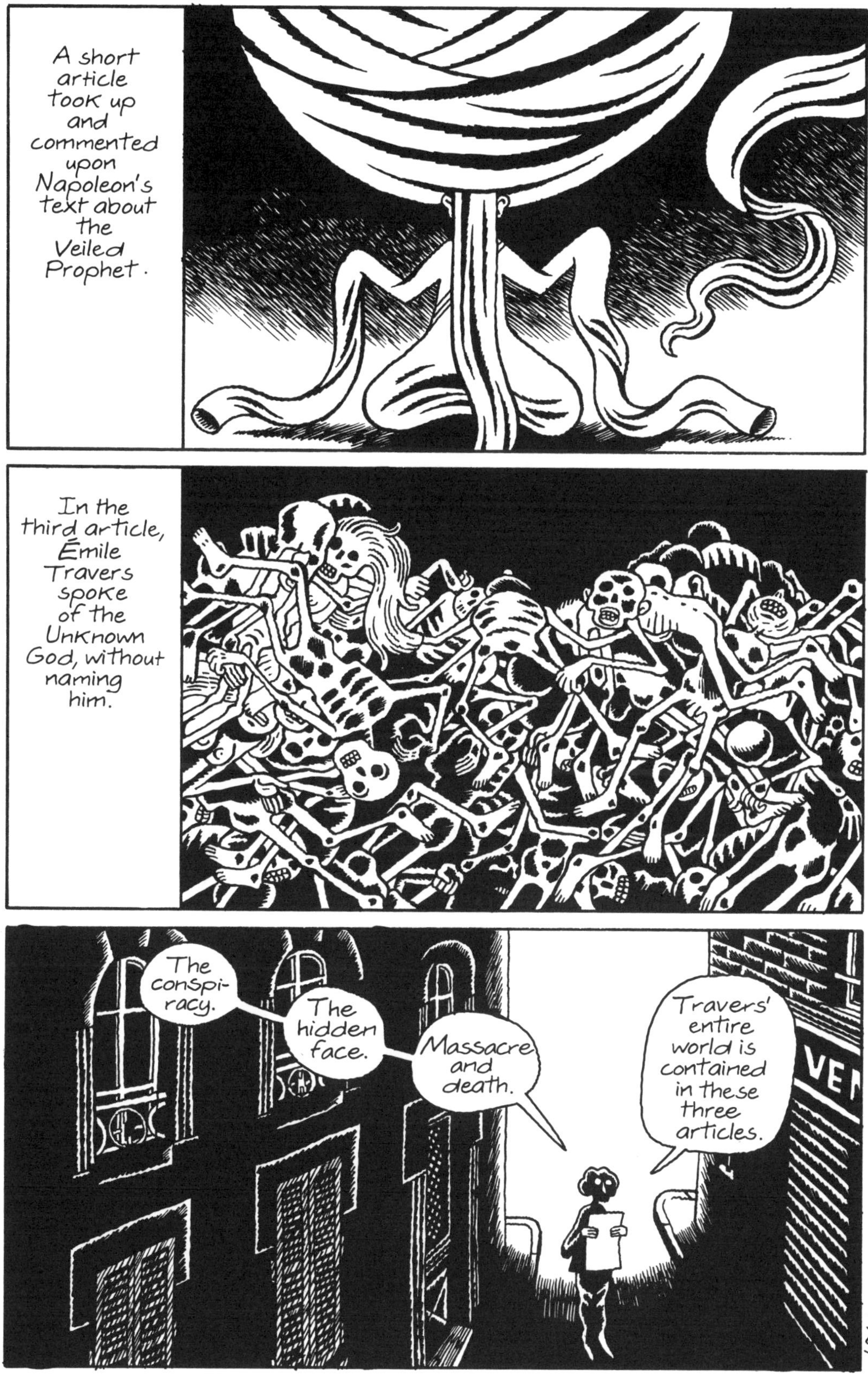
A short article took up and commented upon Napoleon's text about the Veiled Prophet.
In the third article, Émile Travers spoke of the Unknown God, without naming him.
The conspiracy.
The hidden face.
Massacre and death.
Travers' entire world is contained in these three articles.

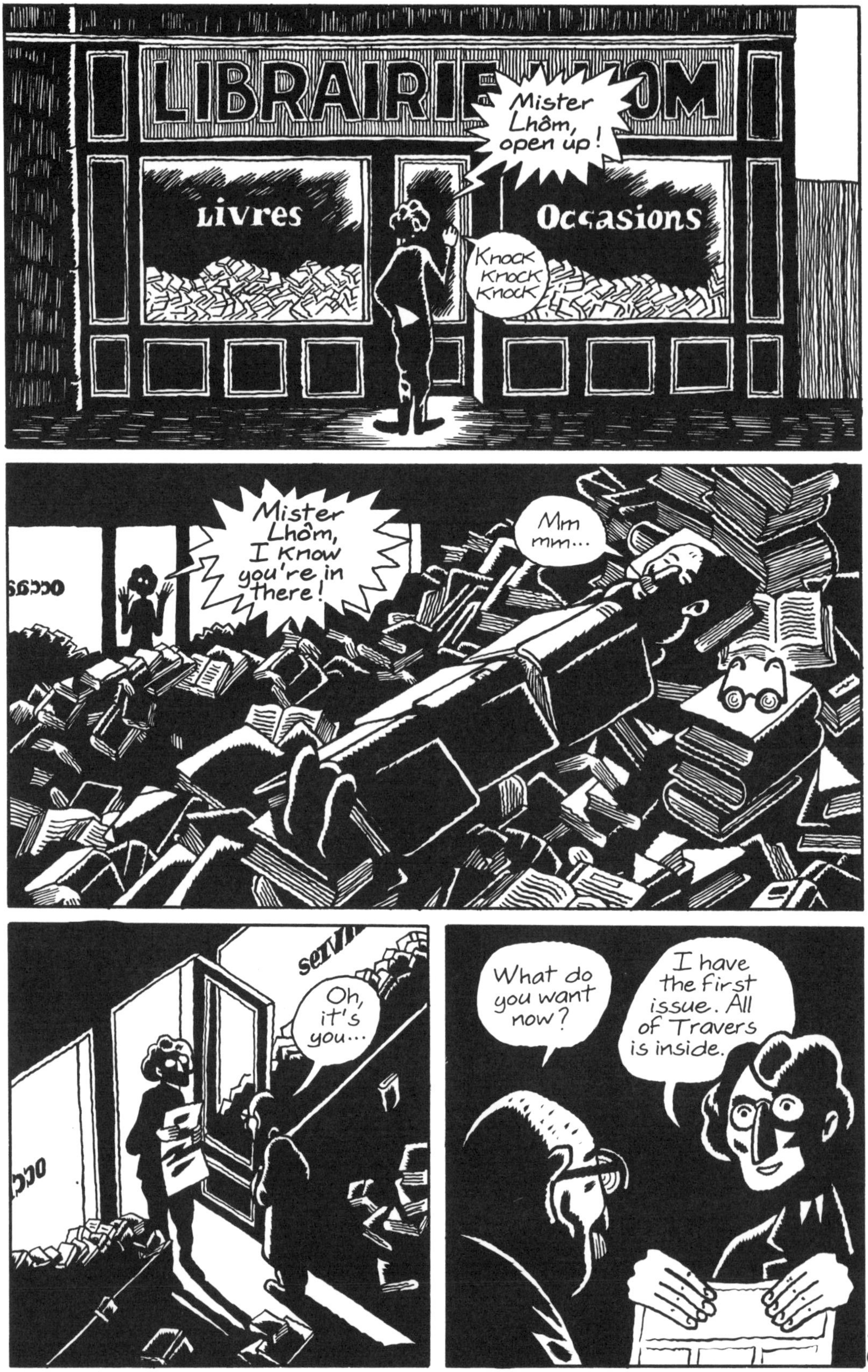

LIBRAIRIE
Mister Lhôm, open up!
Livres
Occasions
Knock Knock Knock
Mister Lhôm, I know you're in there!
Mm mm...
Oh, it's you...
What do you want now?
I have the first issue. All of Travers is inside.

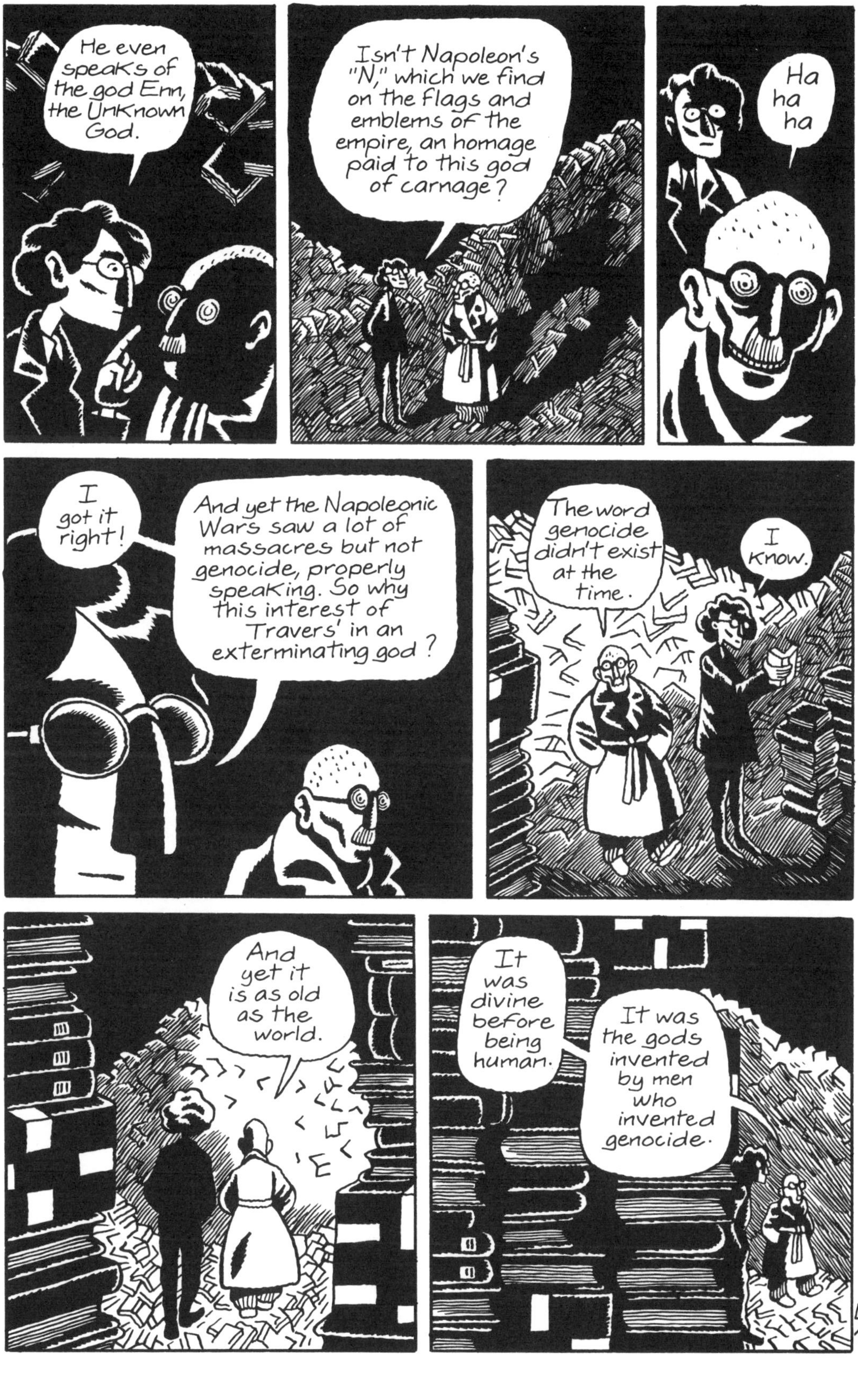
He even speaks of the god Enn, the Unknown God.
Isn't Napoleon's "N," which we find on the flags and emblems of the empire, an homage paid to this god of carnage?
Ha ha ha
I got it right!
And yet the Napoleonic Wars saw a lot of massacres but not genocide, properly speaking. So why this interest of Travers' in an exterminating god?
The word genocide didn't exist at the time.
I know.
And yet it is as old as the world.
It was divine before being human.
It was the gods invented by men who invented genocide.

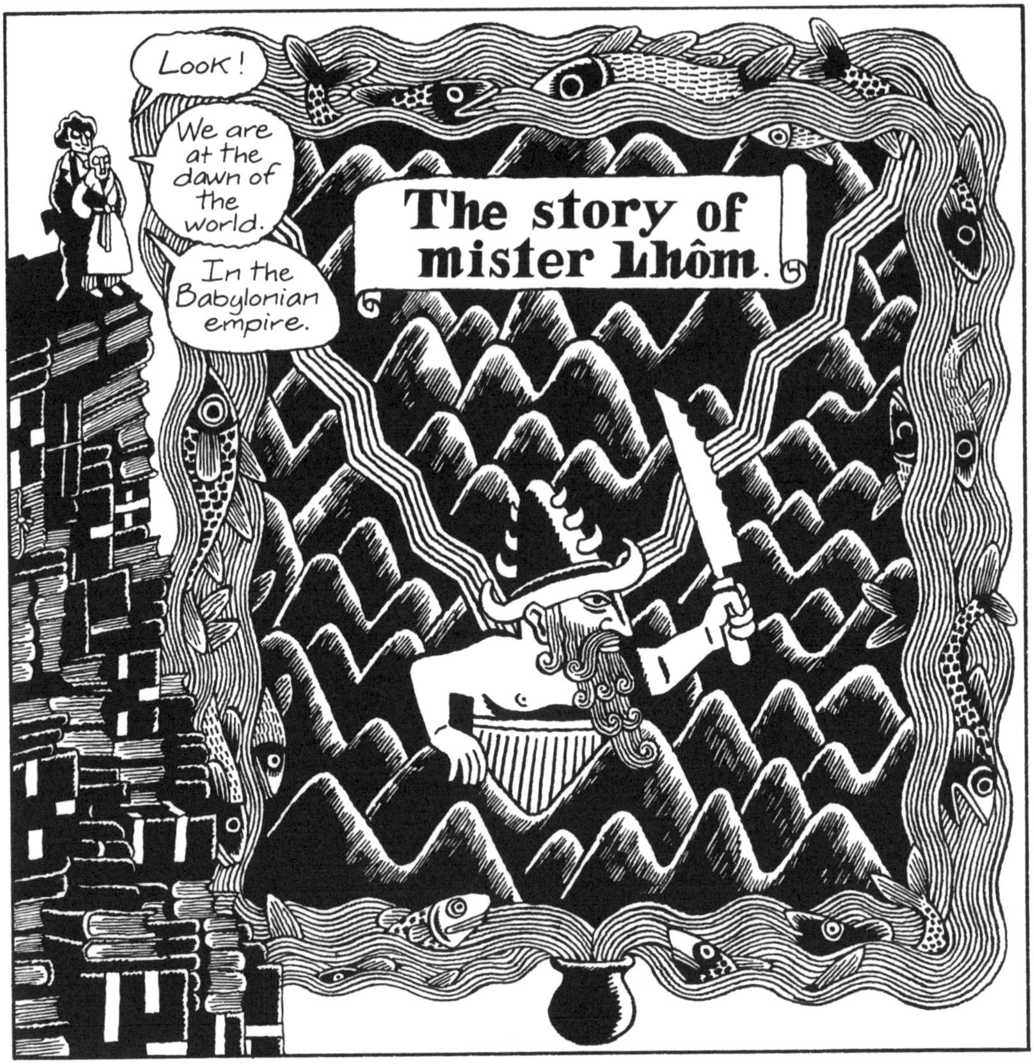
Look!
We are at the dawn of the world.
In the Babylonian empire.
The story of mister Lhôm.

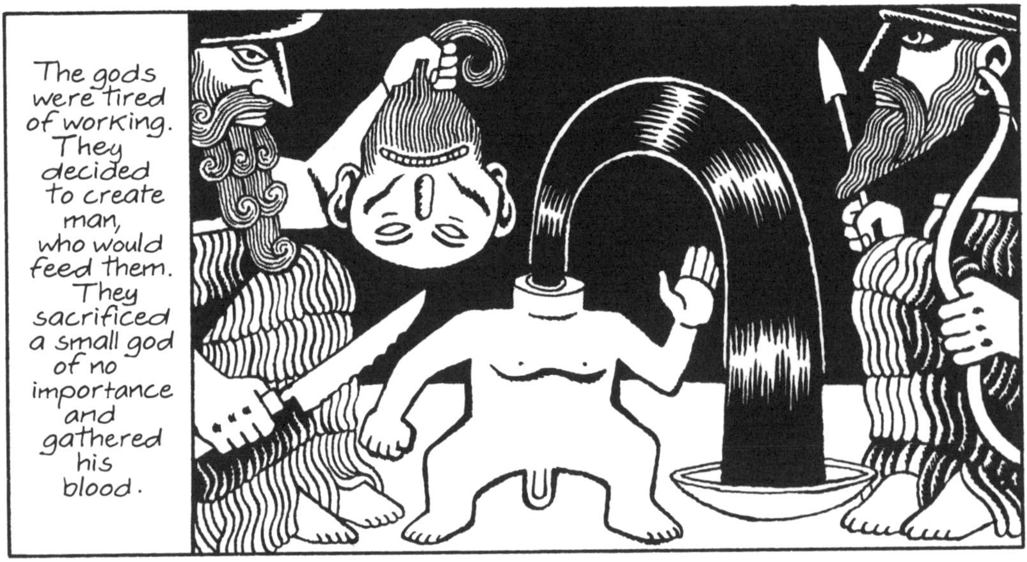
The gods were tired of working. They decided to create man, who would feed them. They sacrificed a small god of no importance and gathered his blood.

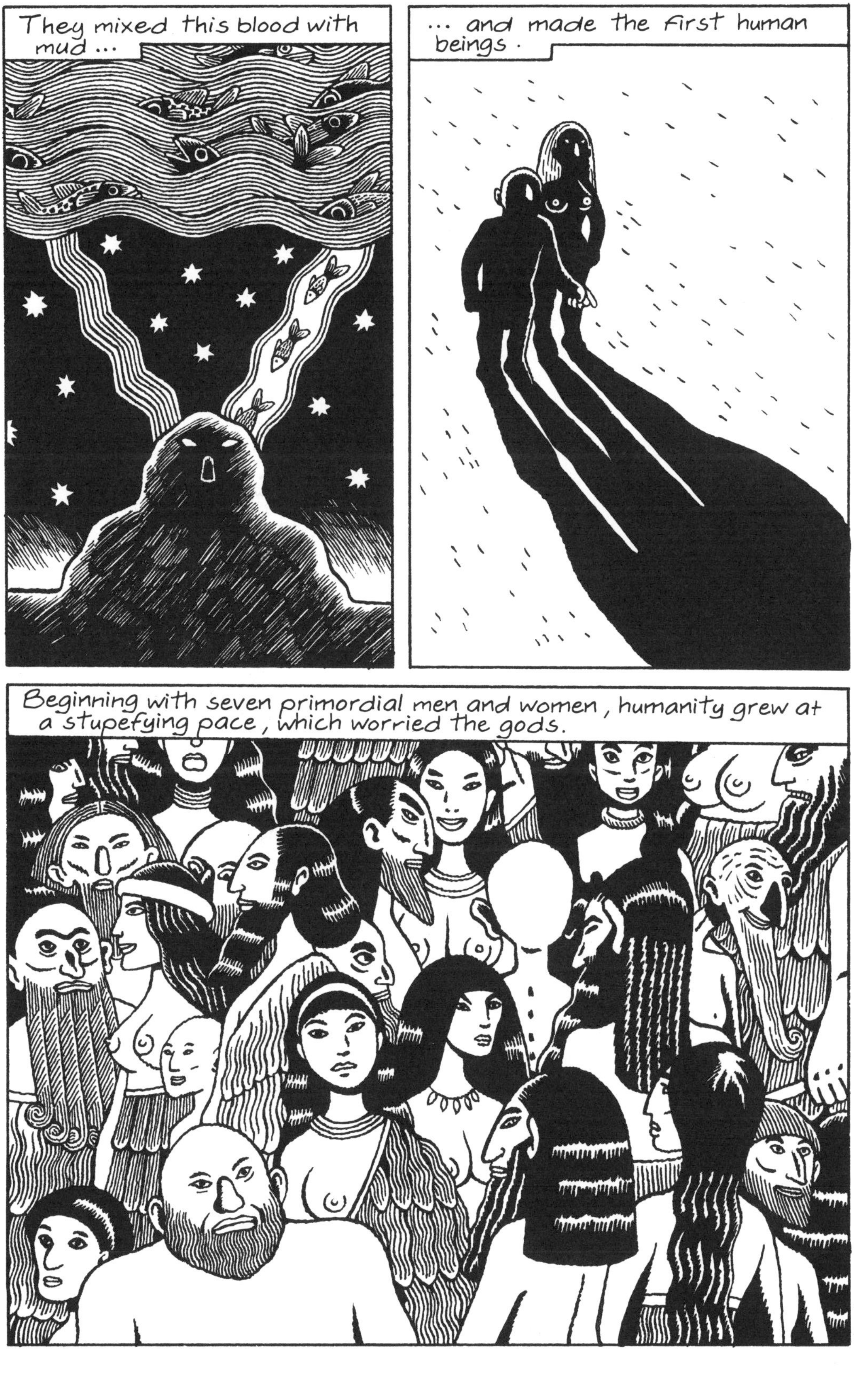
They mixed this blood with mud ...
... and made the first human beings.
Beginning with seven primordial men and women, humanity grew at a stupefying pace, which worried the gods.

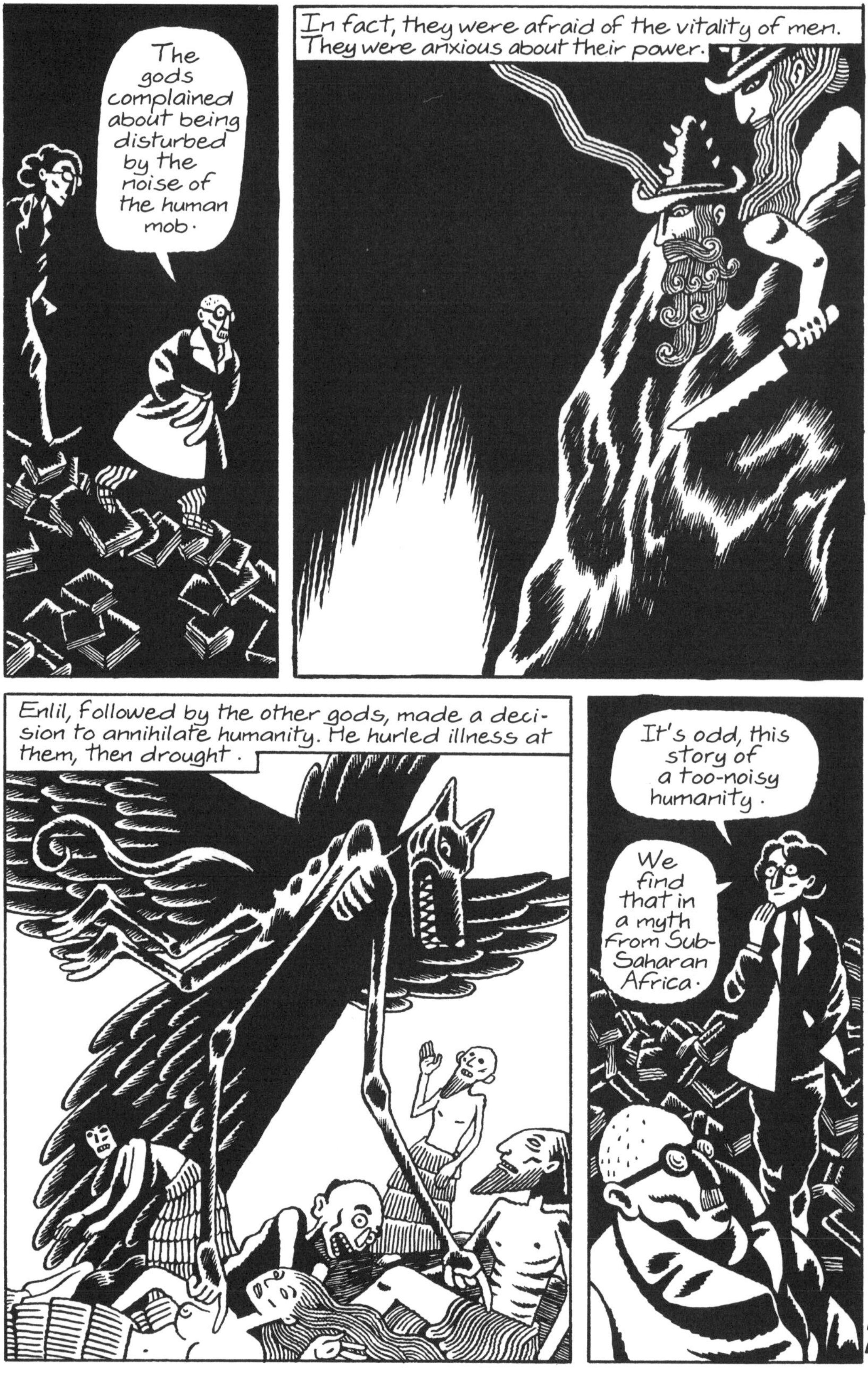
The gods complained about being disturbed by the noise of the human mob.
In fact, they were afraid of the vitality of men. They were anxious about their power.
Enlil, followed by the other gods, made a decision to annihilate humanity. He hurled illness at them, then drought.
It's odd, this story of a too-noisy humanity.
We find that in a myth from Sub-Saharan Africa.

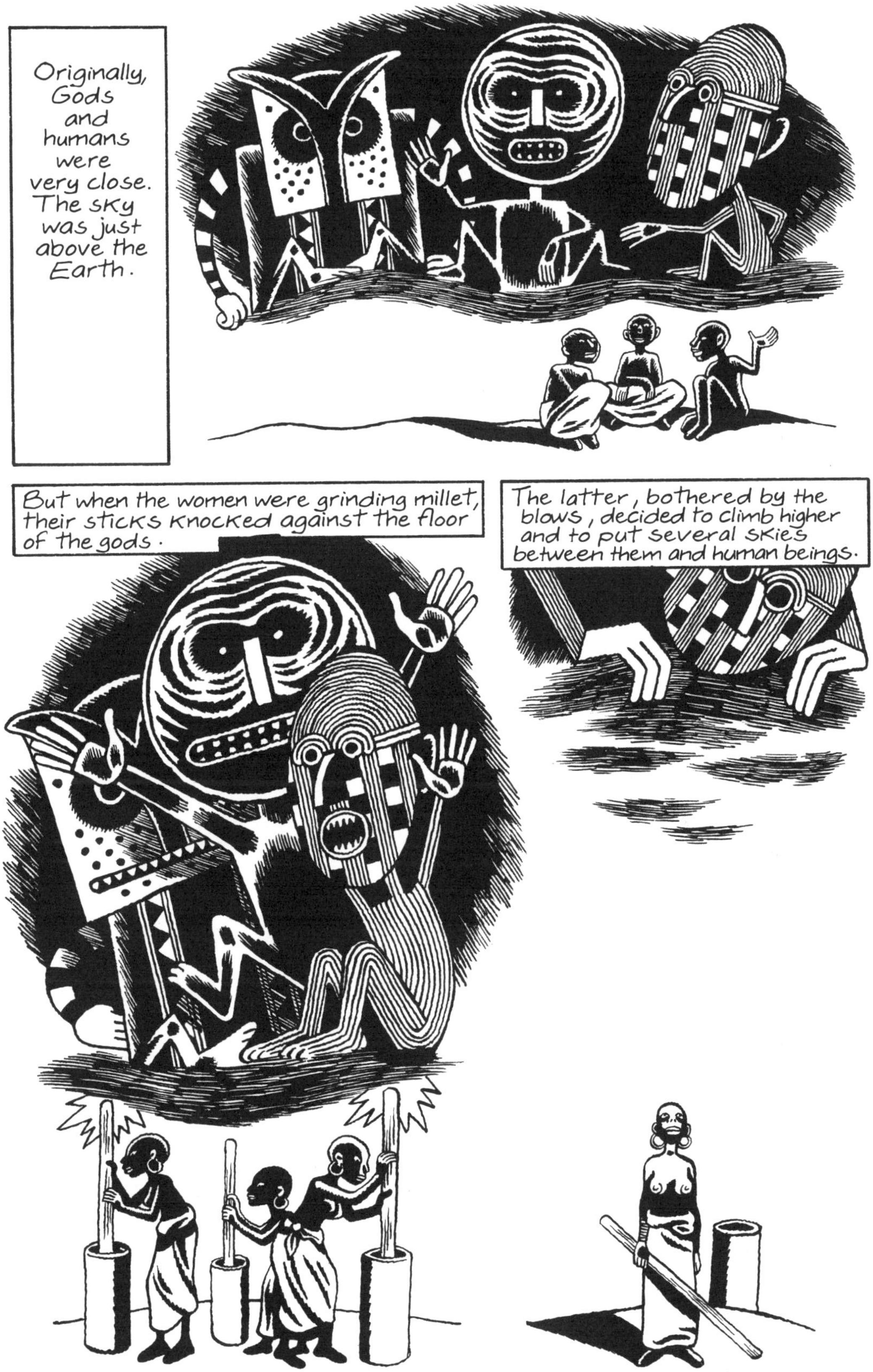
Originally, Gods and humans were very close. The sky was just above the Earth.
But when the women were grinding millet, their sticks knocked against the floor of the gods.
The latter, bothered by the blows, decided to climb higher and to put several skies between them and human beings.

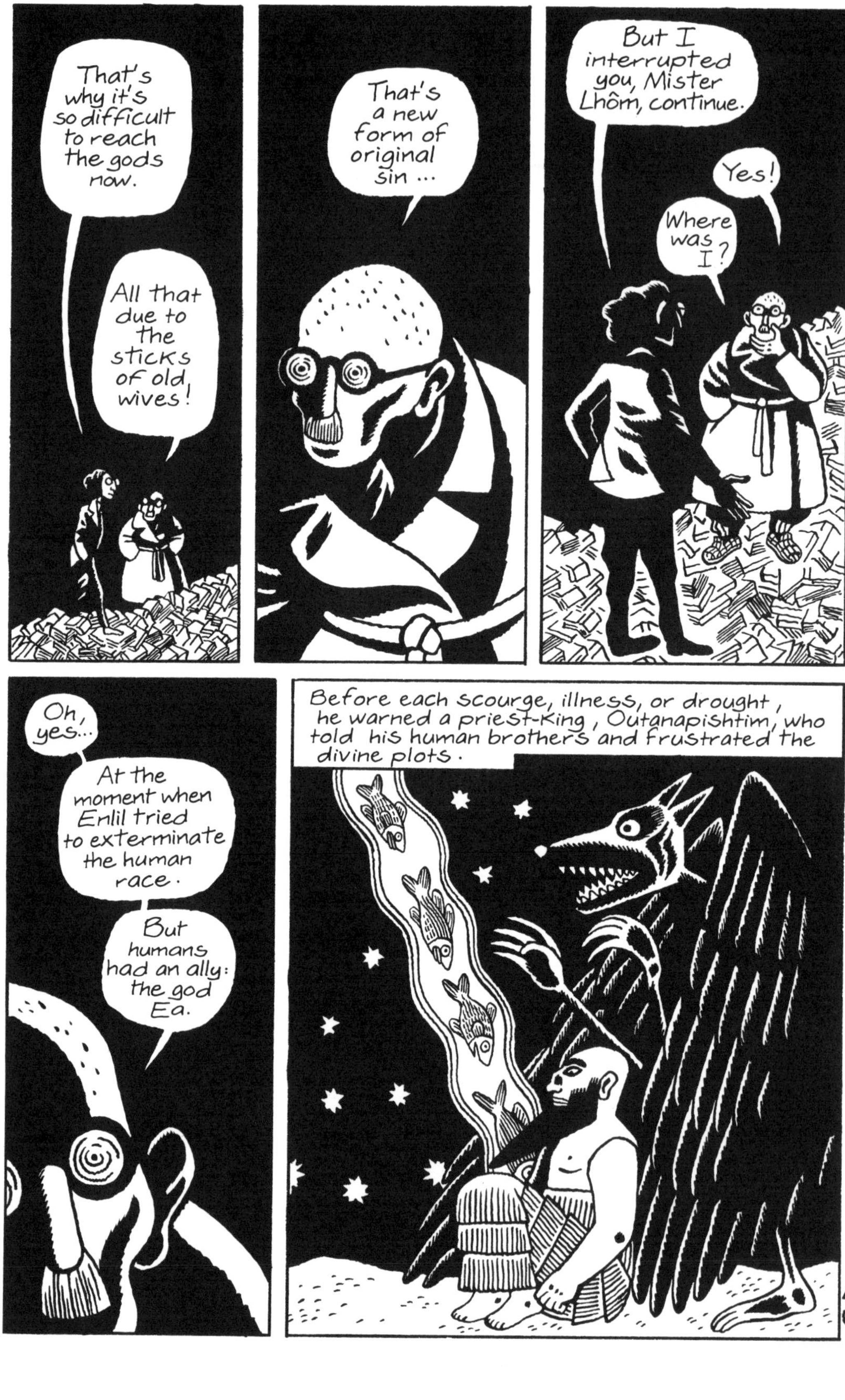
That's why it's so difficult to reach the gods now.
All that due to the sticks of old wives!
That's a new form of original sin ...
But I interrupted you, Mister Lhôm, continue.
Yes!
Where was I?
Oh, yes...
At the moment when Enlil tried to exterminate the human race.
But humans had an ally: the god Ea.
Before each scourge, illness, or drought, he warned a priest-king, Outanapishtim, who told his human brothers and frustrated the divine plots.

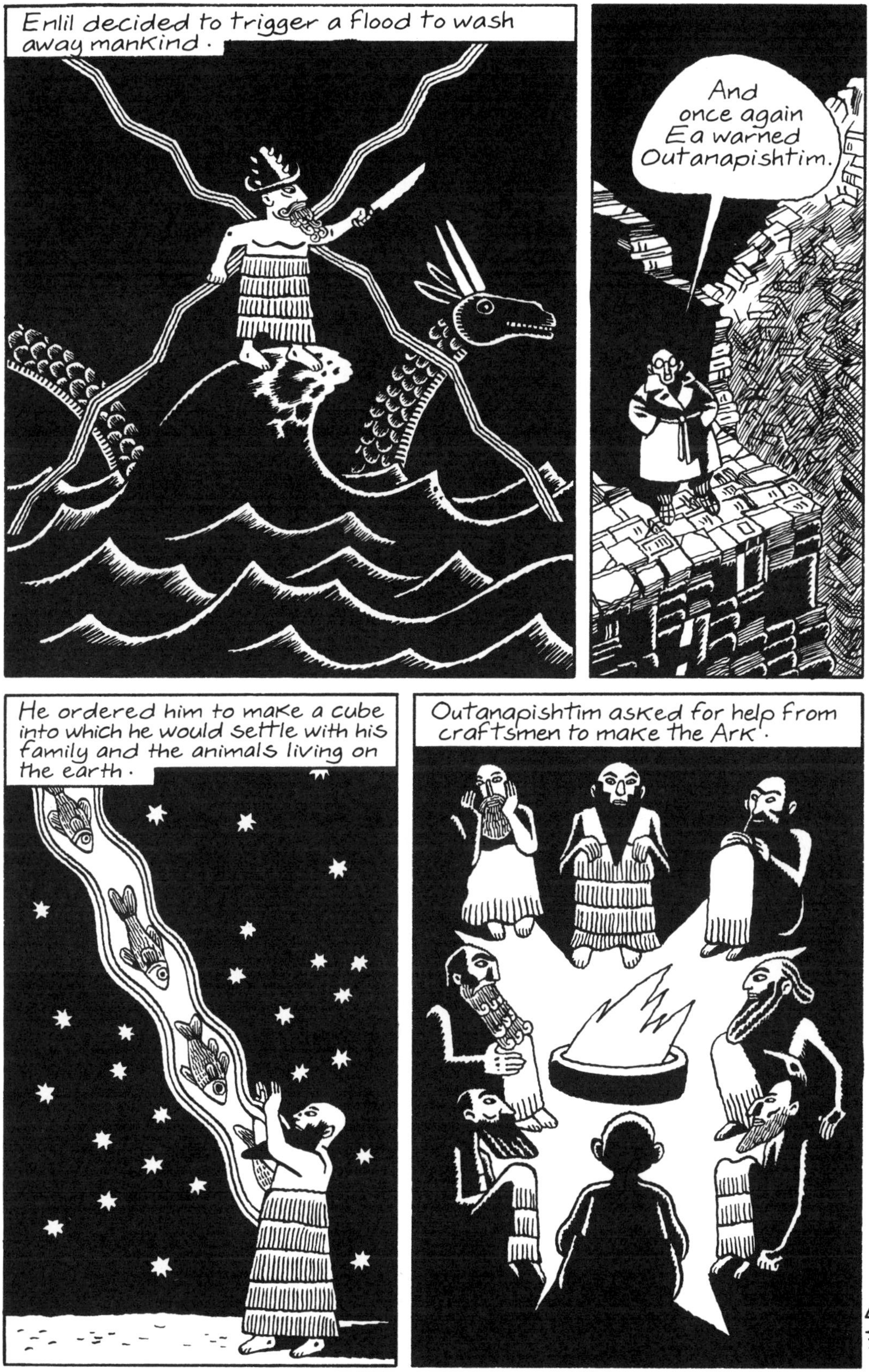
Enlil decided to trigger a flood to wash away mankind.
And once again Ea warned Outanapishtim.
He ordered him to make a cube into which he would settle with his family and the animals living on the earth.
Outanapishtim asked for help from craftsmen to make the Ark.

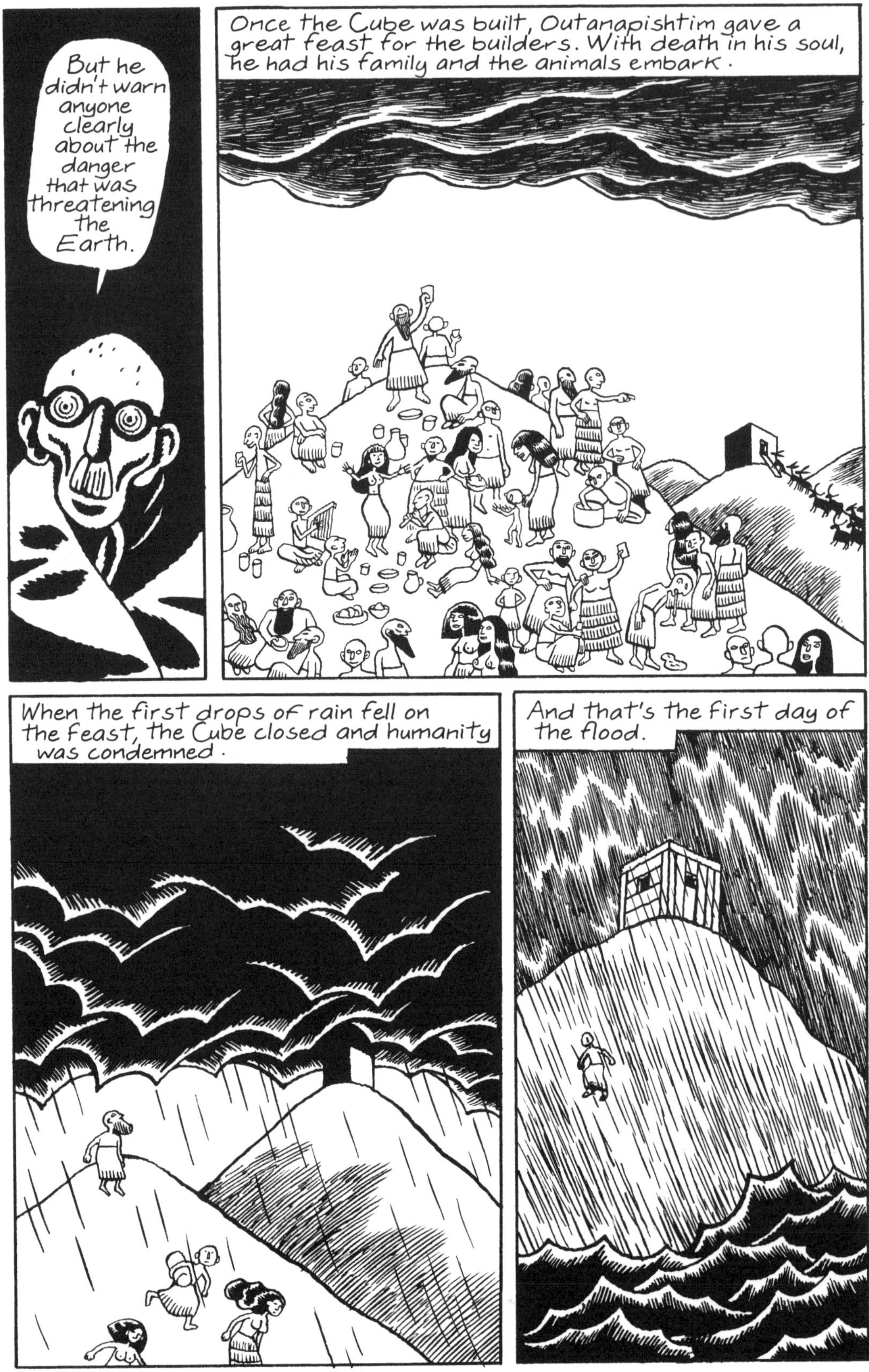

But he didn't warn anyone clearly about the danger that was threatening the Earth.
Once the Cube was built, Outanapishtim gave a great feast for the builders. With death in his soul, he had his family and the animals embark.
When the first drops of rain fell on the feast, the Cube closed and humanity was condemned.
And that's the first day of the flood.

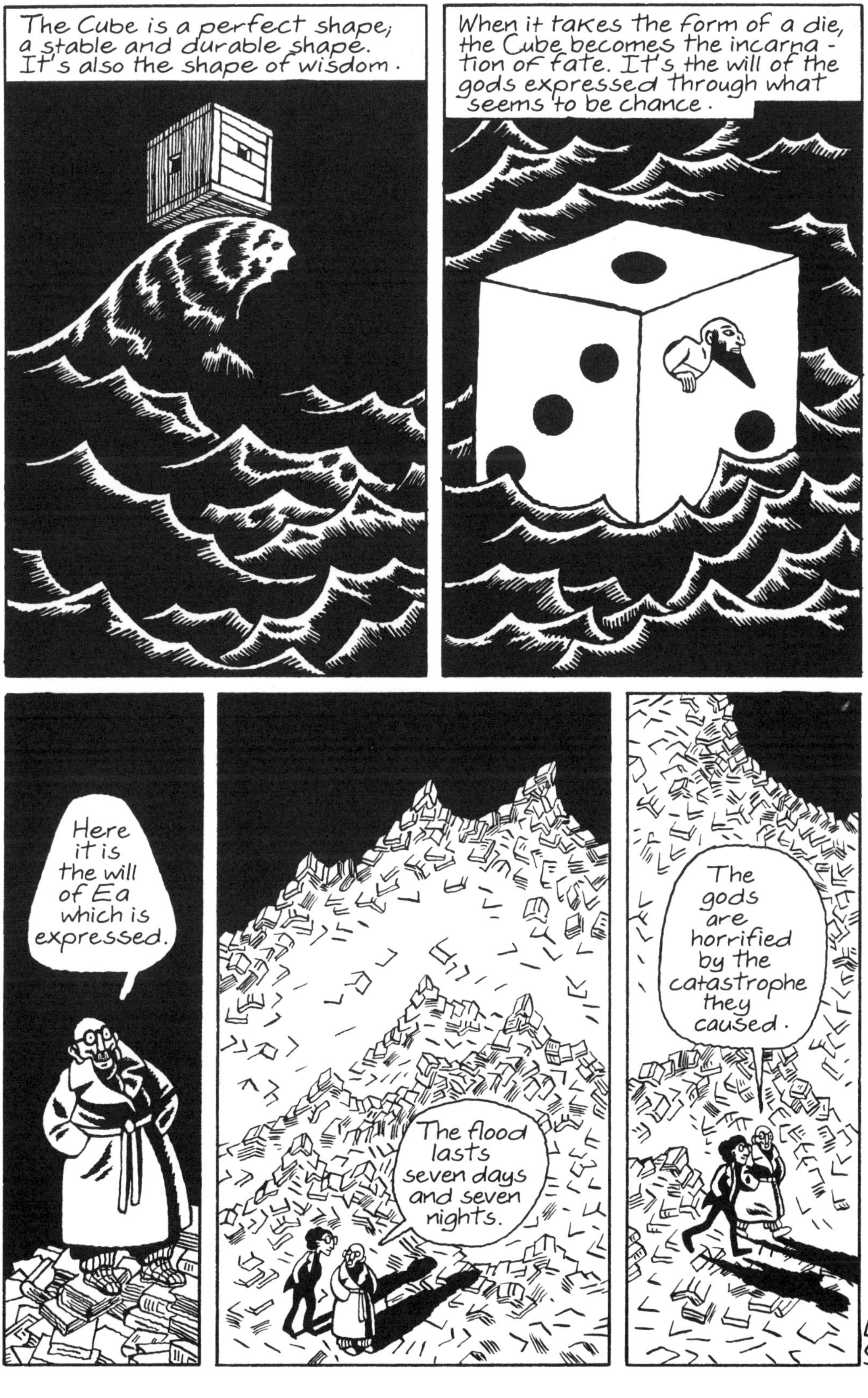
The Cube is a perfect shape; a stable and durable shape. It's also the shape of wisdom.
When it takes the form of a die, the Cube becomes the incarnation of fate. It's the will of the gods expressed through what seems to be chance.
Here it is the will of Ea which is expressed.
The flood lasts seven days and seven nights.
The gods are horrified by the catastrophe they caused.

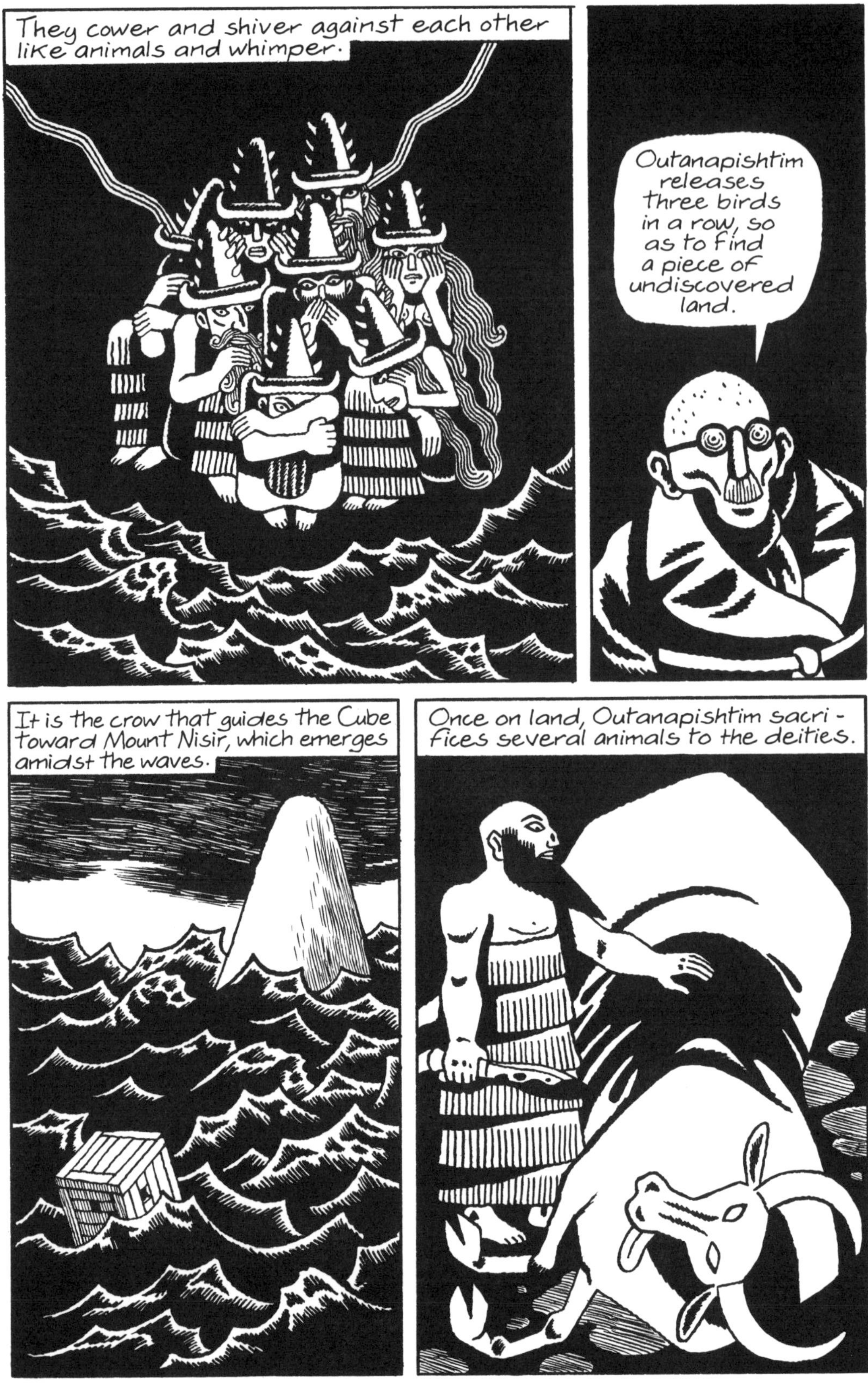
They cower and shiver against each other like animals and whimper.
Outanapishtim releases three birds in a row, so as to find a piece of undiscovered land.
It is the crow that guides the Cube toward Mount Nisir, which emerges amidst the waves.
Once on land, Outanapishtim sacri - fices several animals to the deities.

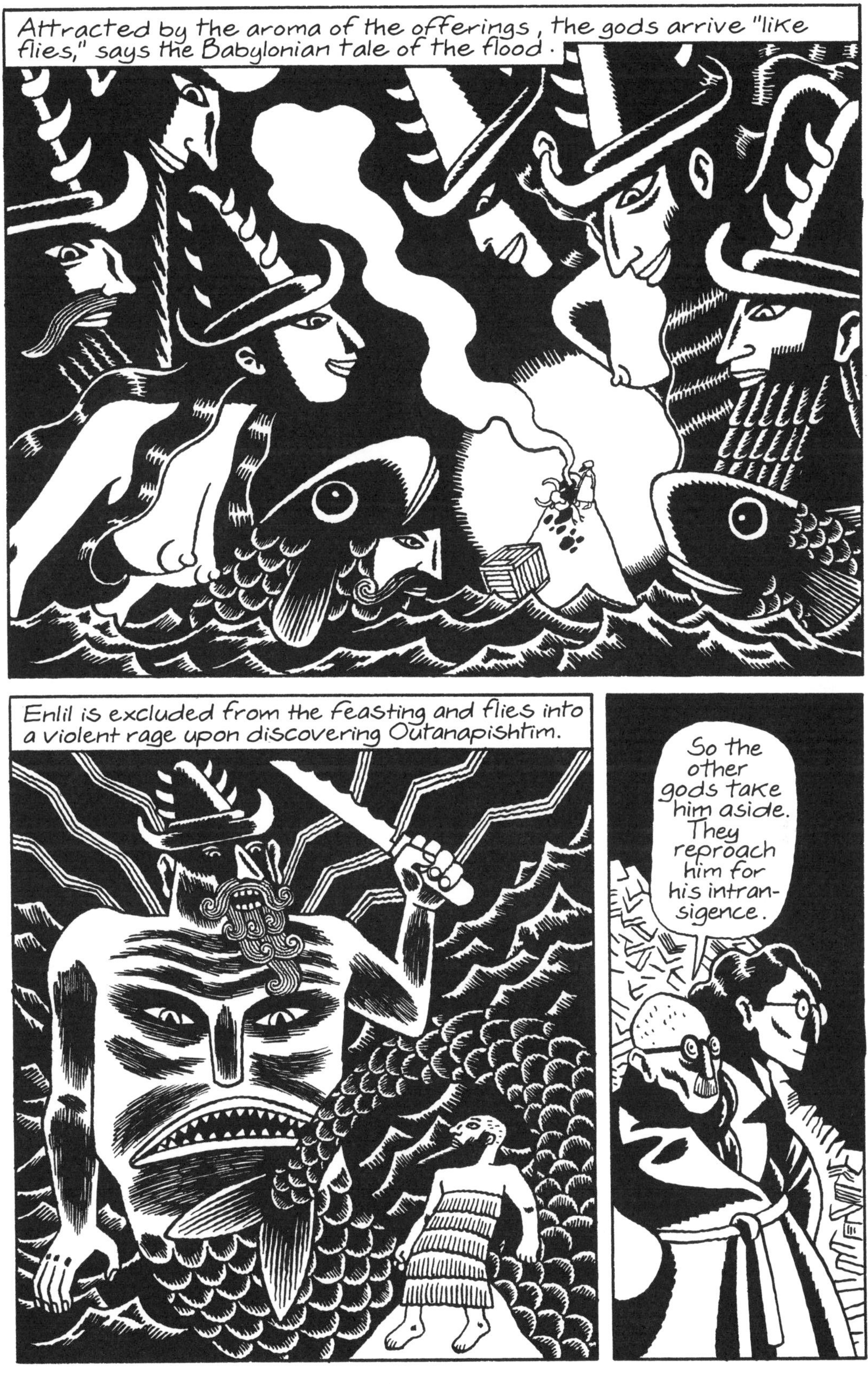
Attracted by the aroma of the offerings, the gods arrive "like flies," says the Babylonian tale of the flood.
Enlil is excluded from the feasting and flies into a violent rage upon discovering Outanapishtim.
So the other gods take him aside. They reproach him for his intransigence.

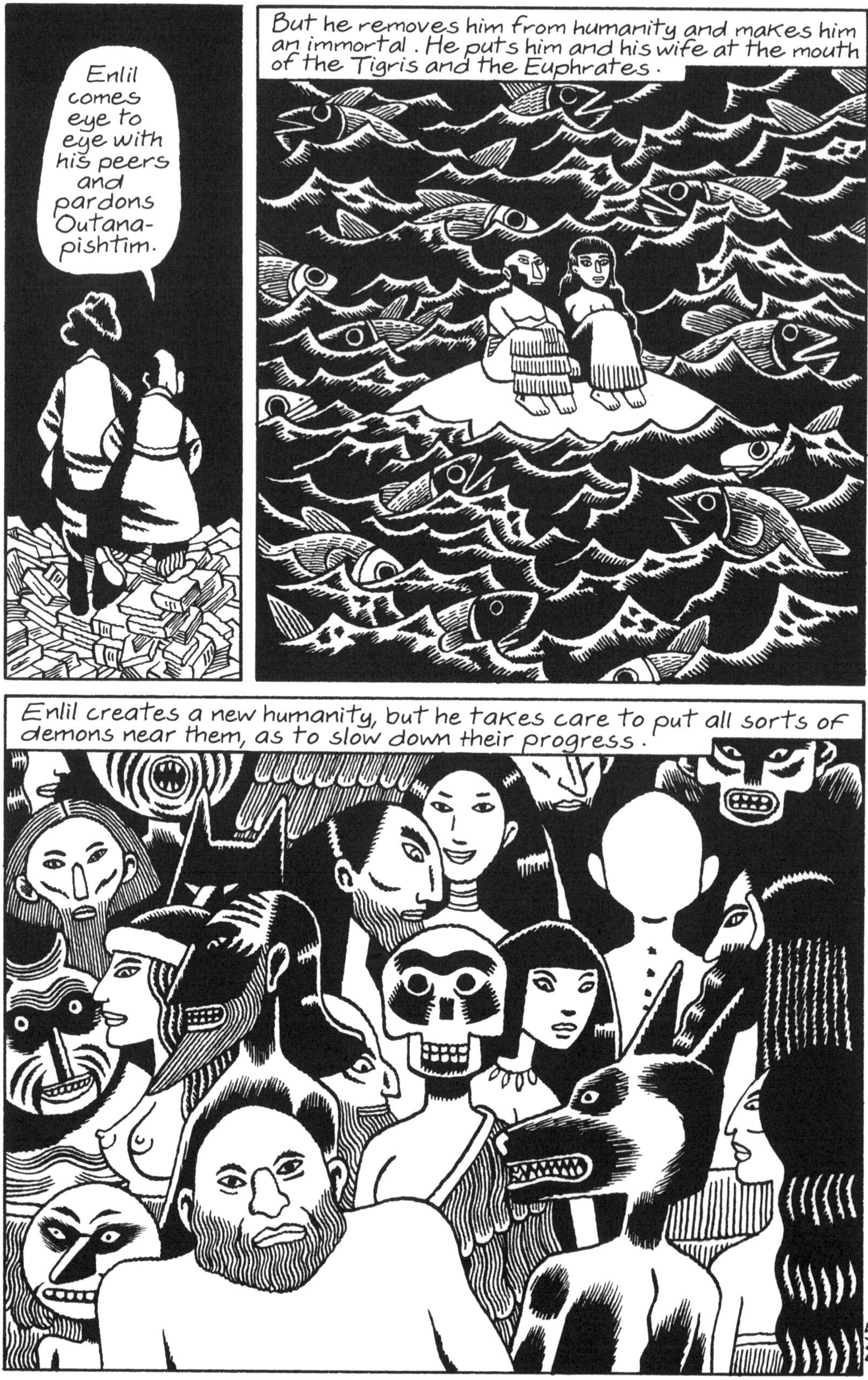
Enlil comes eye to eye with his peers and pardons Outanapishtim.
But he removes him from humanity and makes him an immortal. He puts him and his wife at the mouth of the Tigris and the Euphrates.
Enlil creates a new humanity, but he takes care to put all sorts of demons near them, as to slow down their progress.

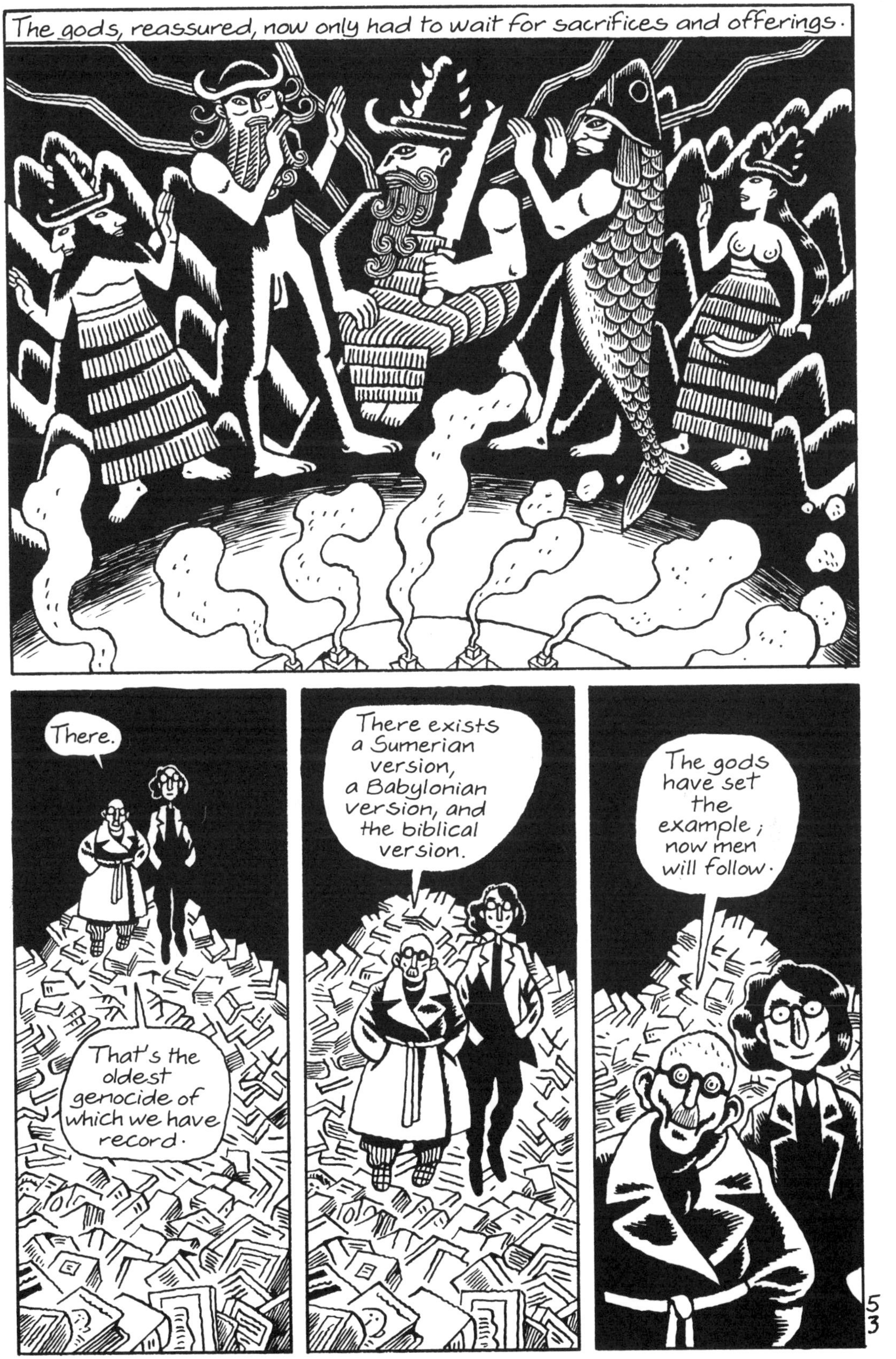
The gods, reassured, now only had to wait for sacrifices and offerings.
There.
That's the oldest genocide of which we have record.
There exists a Sumerian version, a Babylonian version, and the biblical version.
The gods have set the example; now men will follow.

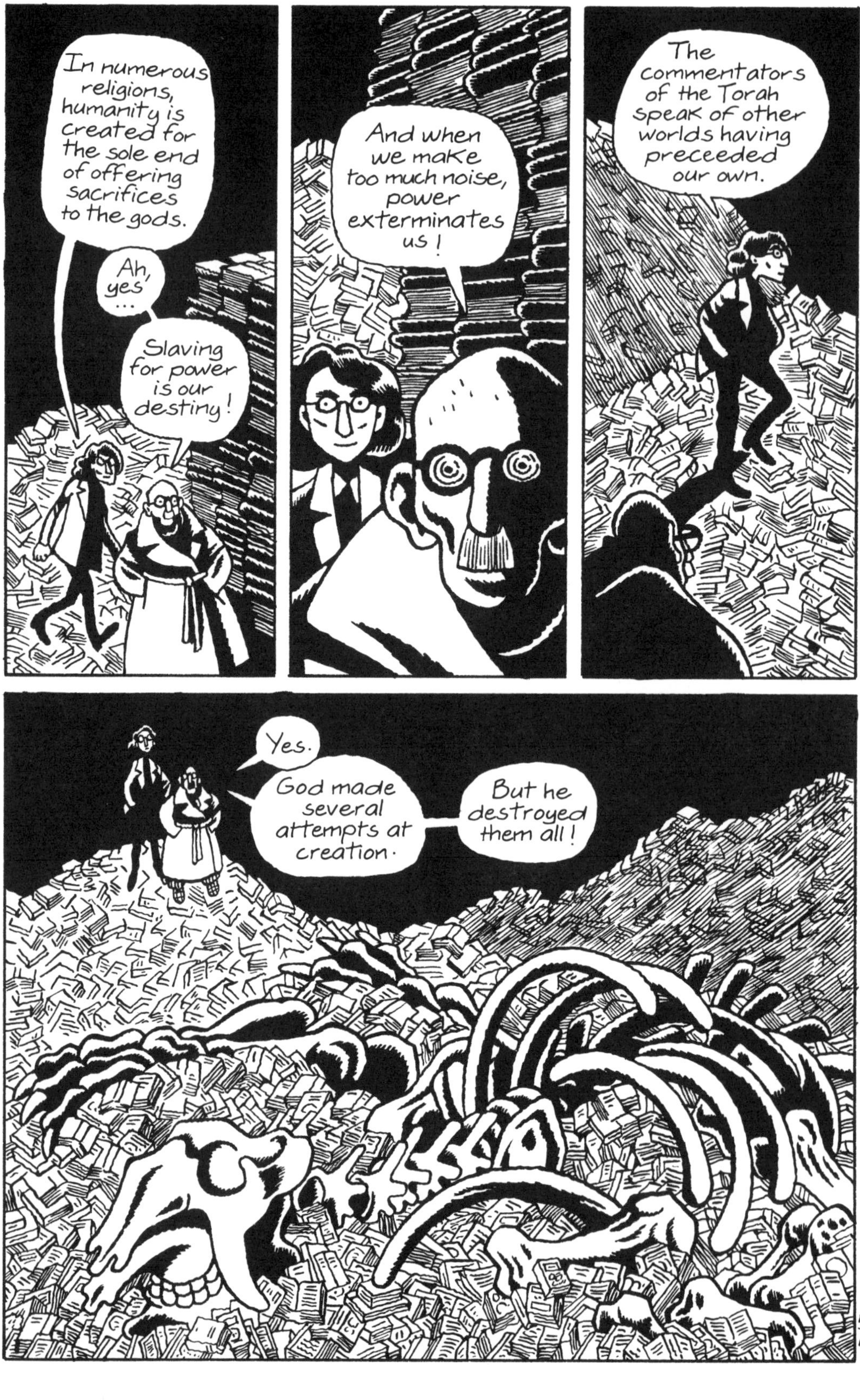
In numerous religions, humanity is created for the sole end of offering sacrifices to the gods.
Ah, yes ...
Slaving for power is our destiny!
And when we make too much noise, power exterminates us!
The commentators of the Torah speak of other worlds having preceeded our own.
Yes.
God made several attempts at creation.
But he destroyed them all!

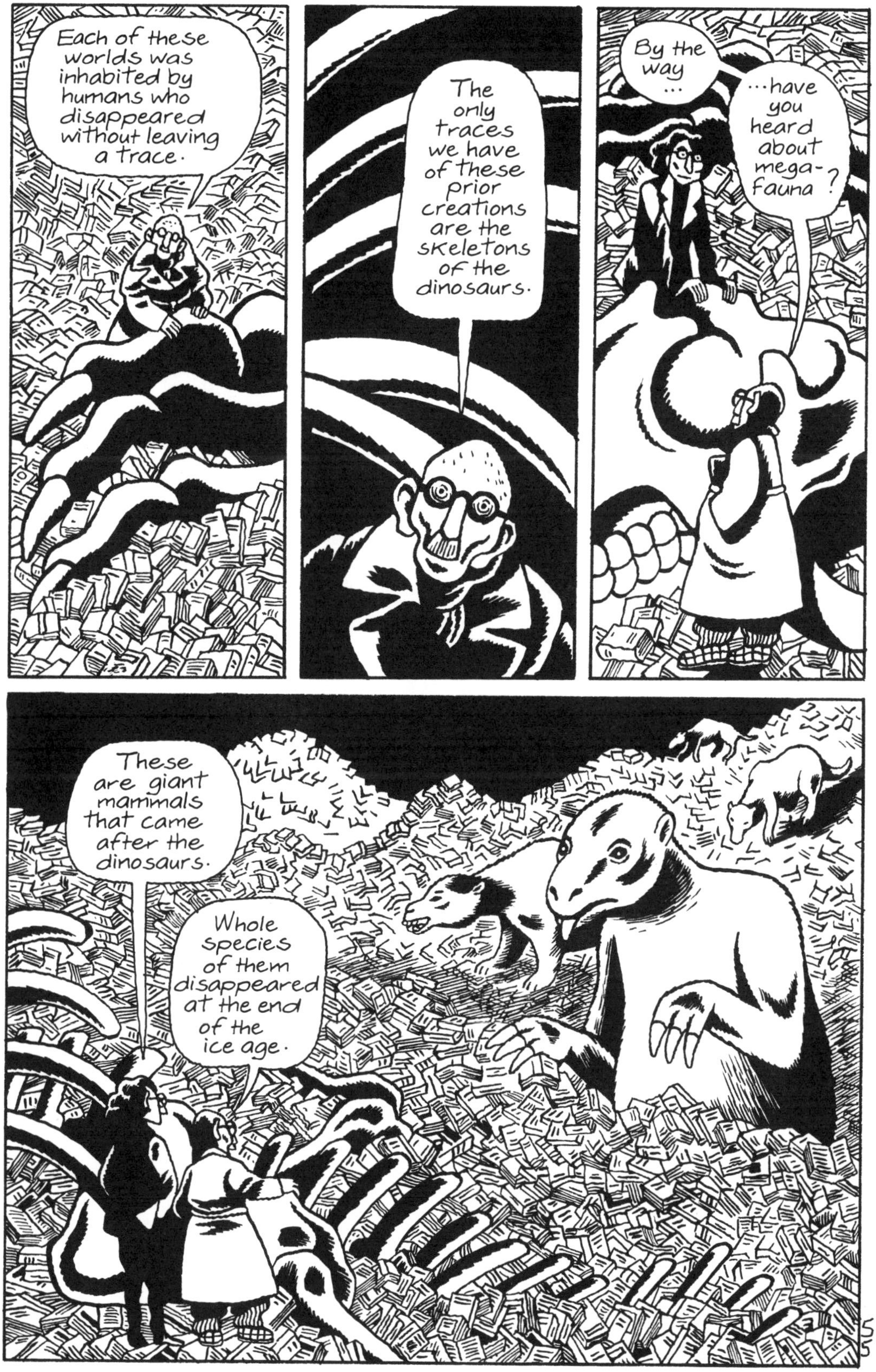

Each of these worlds was inhabited by humans who disappeared without leaving a trace.
The only traces we have of these prior creations are the skeletons of the dinosaurs.
By the way ...
...have you heard about mega-fauna?
These are giant mammals that came after the dinosaurs.
Whole species of them disappeared at the end of the ice age.

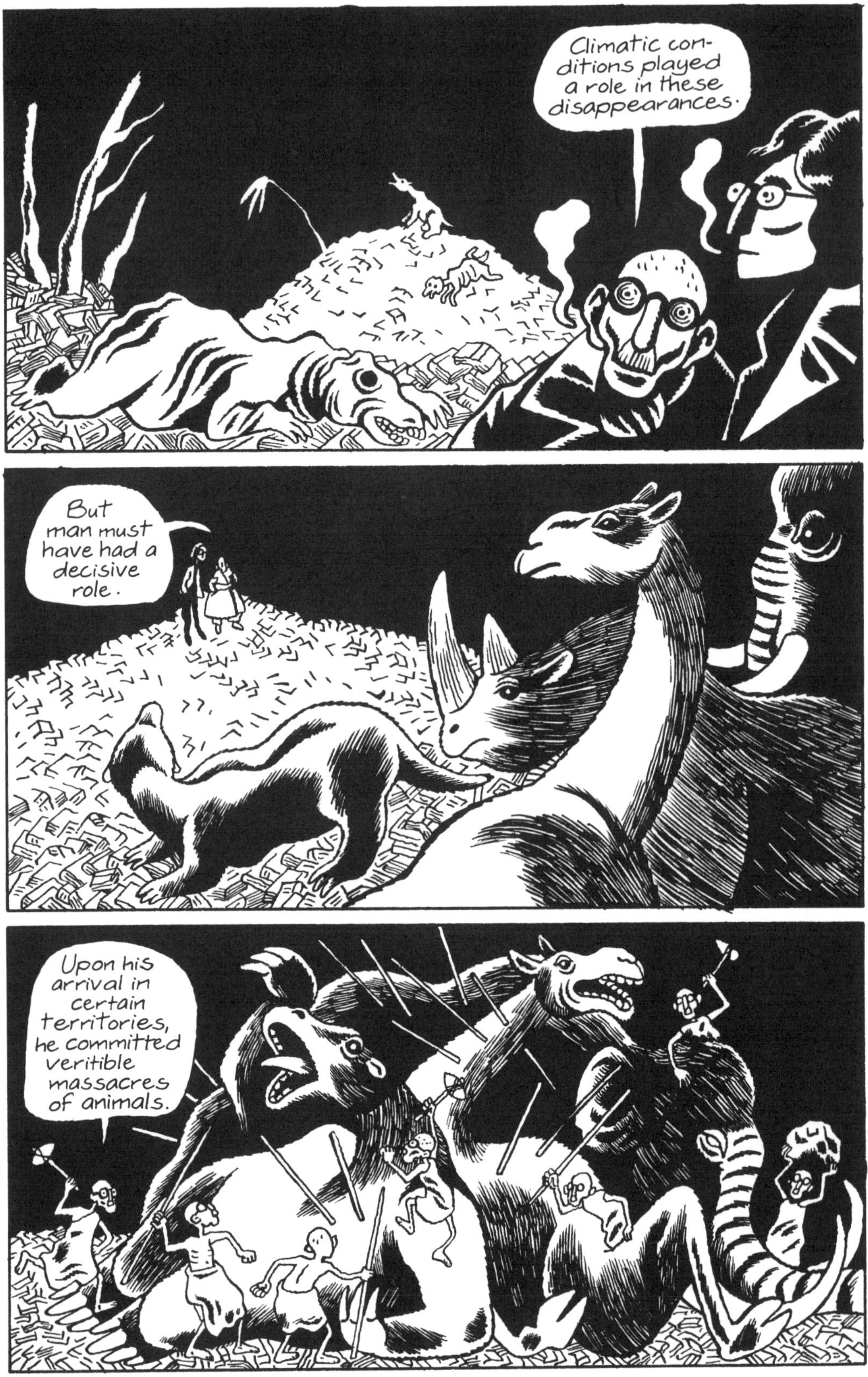
Climatic conditions played a role in these disappearances.
But man must have had a decisive role.
Upon his arrival in certain territories, he committed veritible massacres of animals.

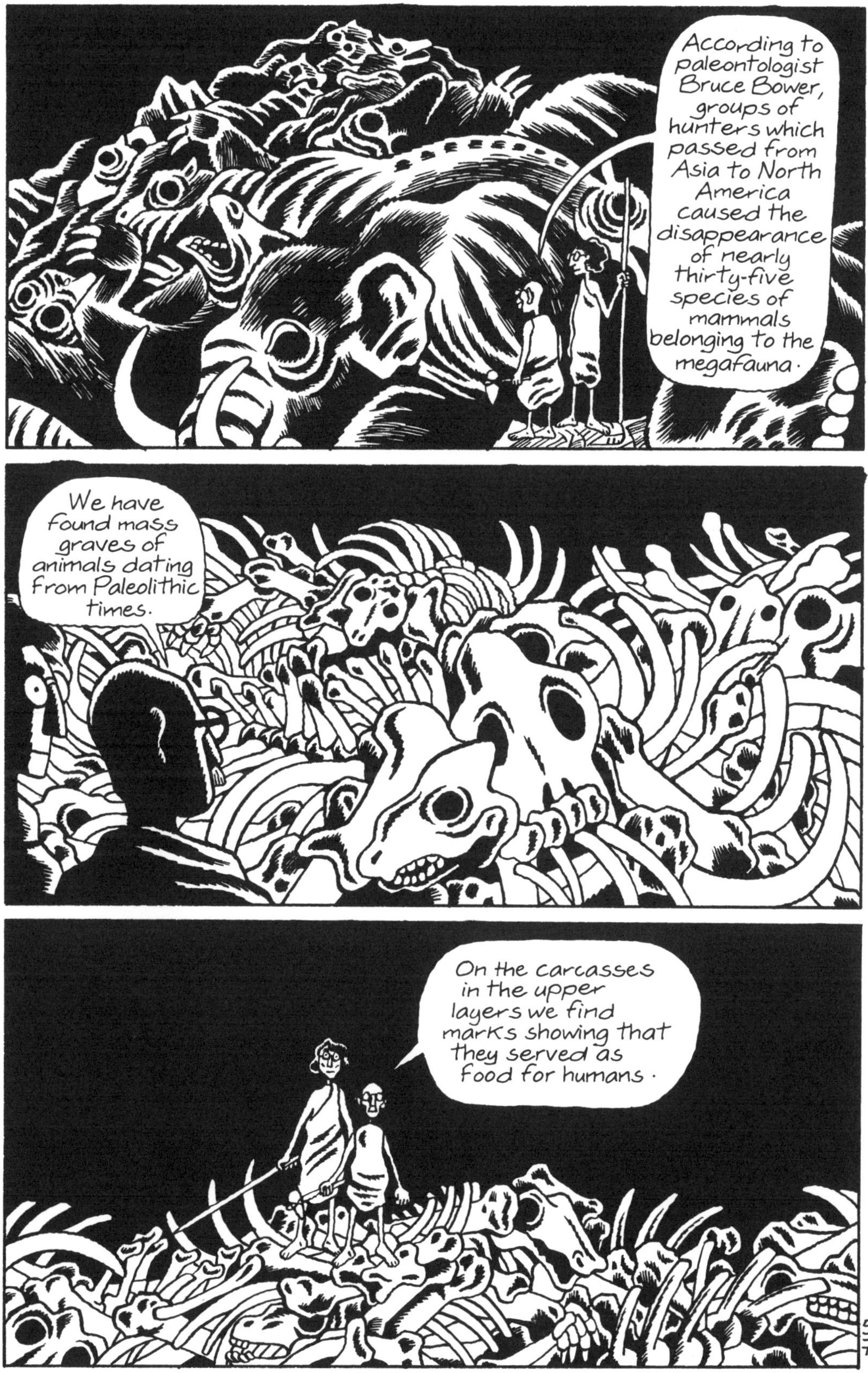
According to paleontologist Bruce Bower, groups of hunters which passed from Asia to North America caused the disappearance of nearly thirty-five species of mammals belonging to the megafauna.
We have found mass graves of animals dating from Paleolithic times.
On the carcasses in the upper layers we find marks showing that they served as food for humans.

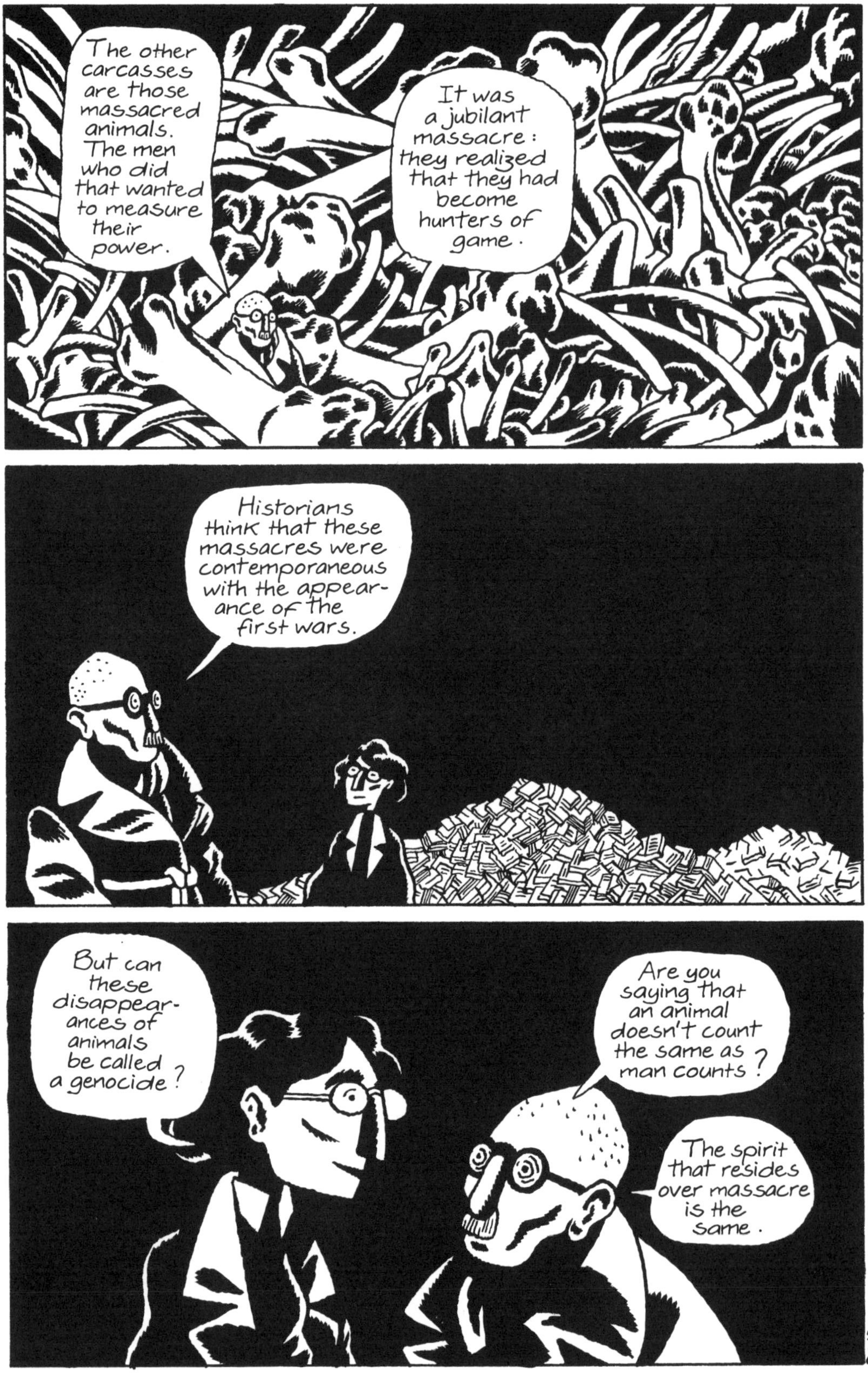
The other carcasses are those massacred animals. The men who did that wanted to measure their power.
It was a jubilant massacre: they realized that they had become hunters of game.
Historians think that these massacres were contemporaneous with the appearance of the first wars.
But can these disappearances of animals be called a genocide?
Are you saying that an animal doesn't count the same as man counts?
The spirit that resides over massacre is the same.

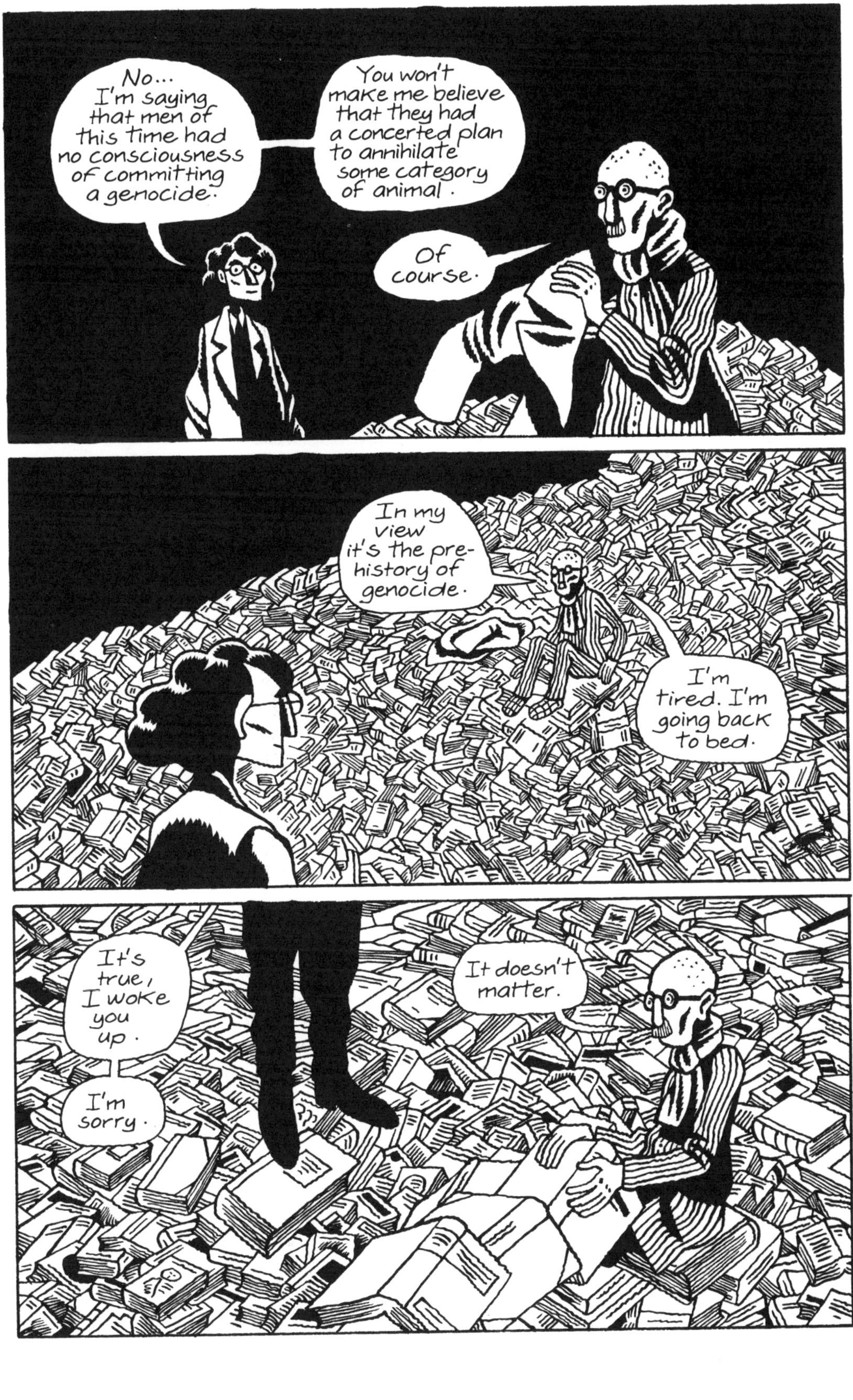
No... I'm saying that men of this time had no consciousness of committing a genocide.
You won't make me believe that they had a concerted plan to annihilate some category of animal.
Of course.
In my view it's the pre-history of genocide.
I'm tired. I'm going back to bed.
It's true, I woke you up.
I'm sorry.
It doesn't matter.

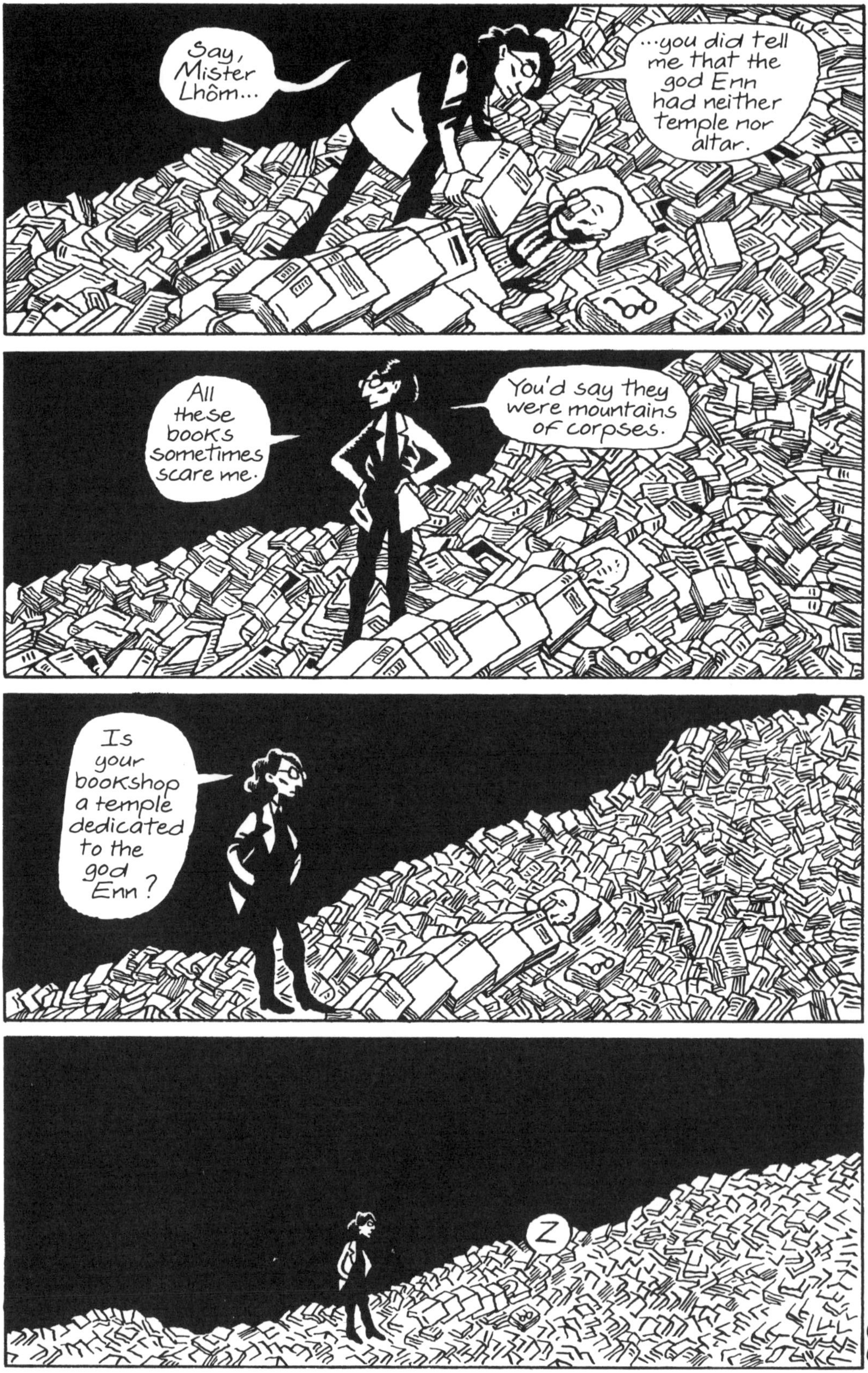
Say, Mister Lhôm...
...you did tell me that the god Enn had neither temple nor altar.
All these books sometimes scare me.
You'd say they were mountains of corpses.
Is your bookshop a temple dedicated to the god Enn?
Z

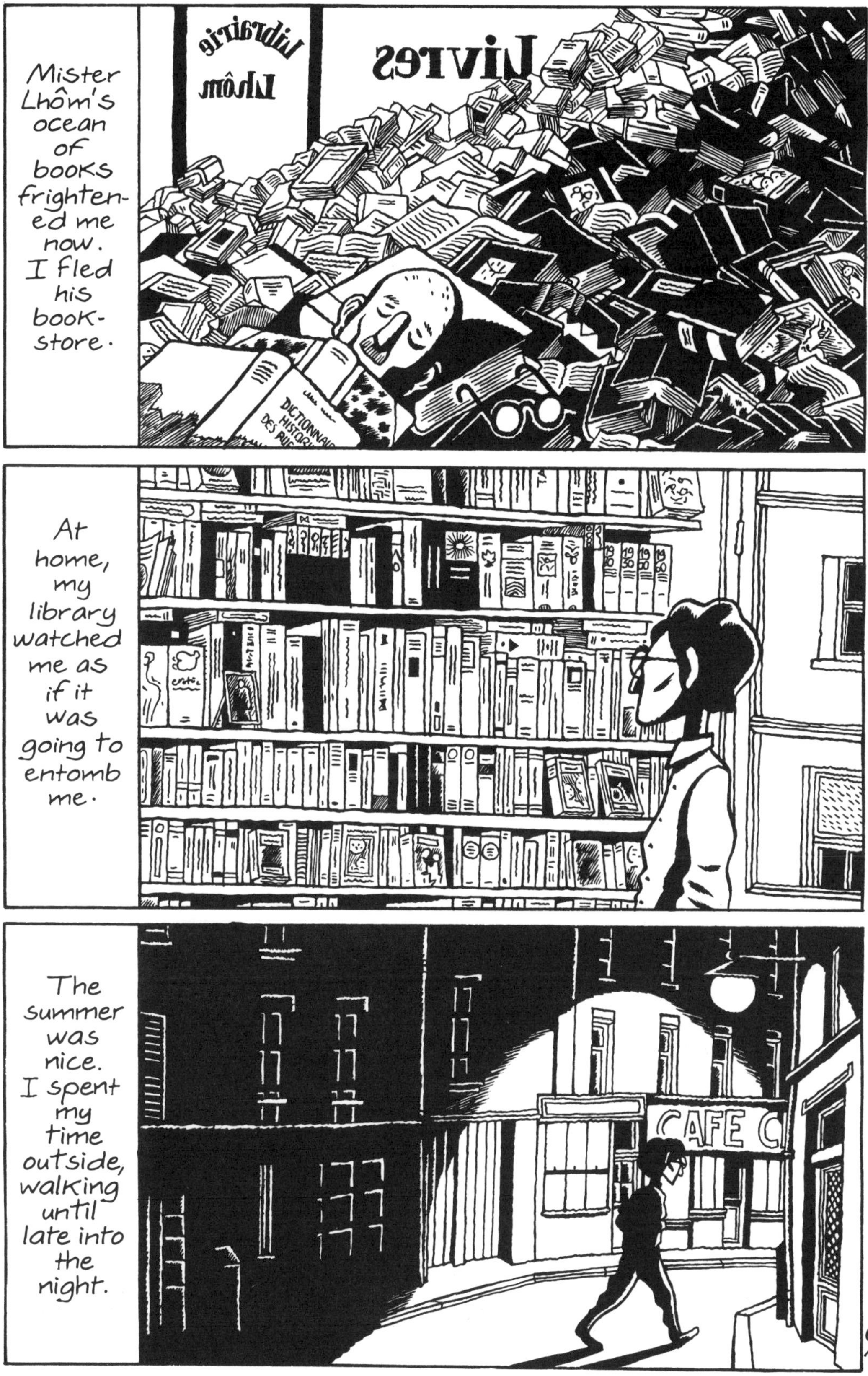

Mister Lhôm's ocean of books frighten-ed me now. I fled his book-store.
Librairie Lhôm
Livres
At home, my library watched me as if it was going to entomb me.
The summer was nice. I spent my time outside, walking until late into the night.
CAFE C

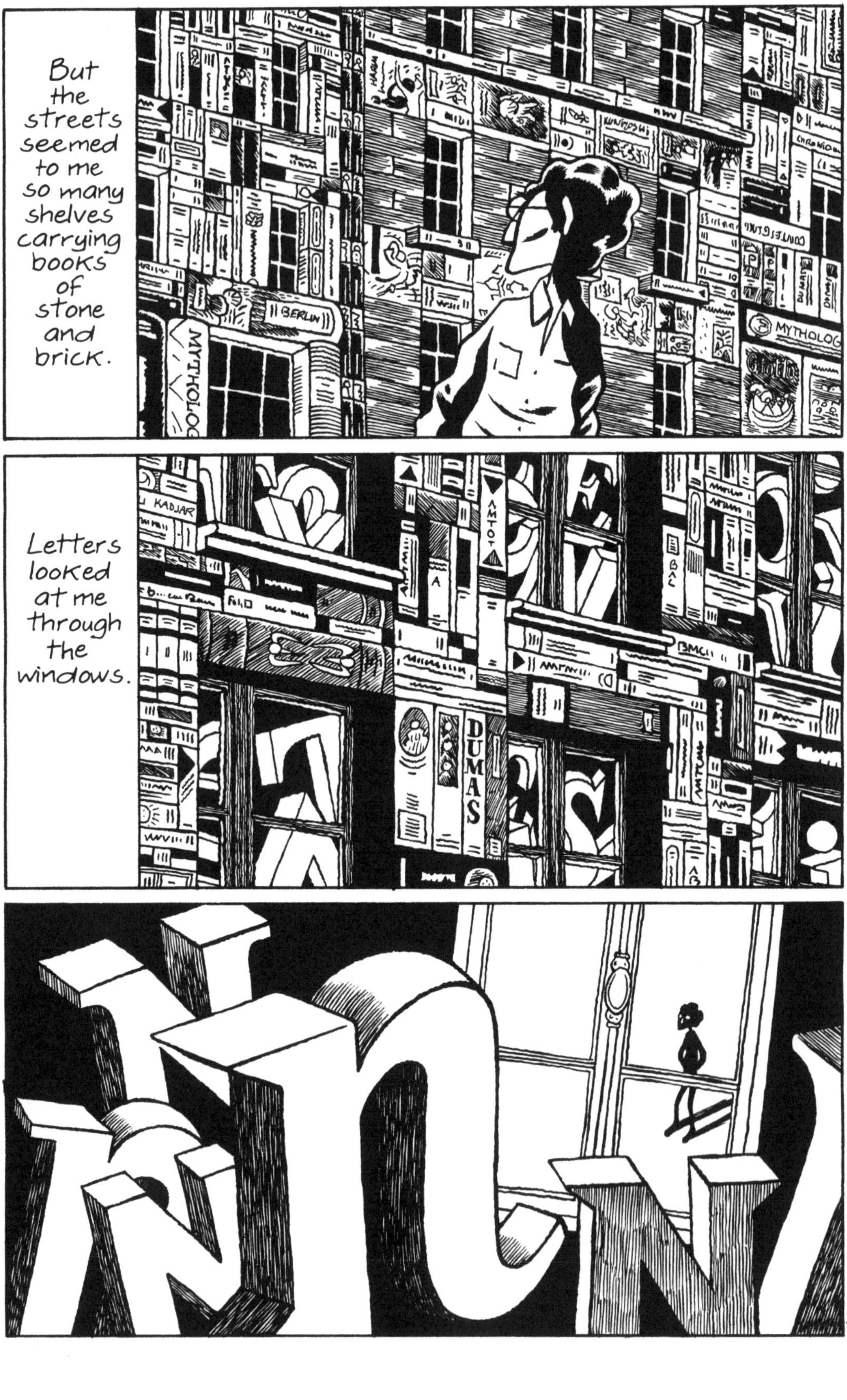
But the streets seemed to me so many shelves carrying books of stone and brick.
BERLIN
MYTHOLOG
MYTHOLOG
Letters looked at me through the windows.
KADJAR
DUMAS

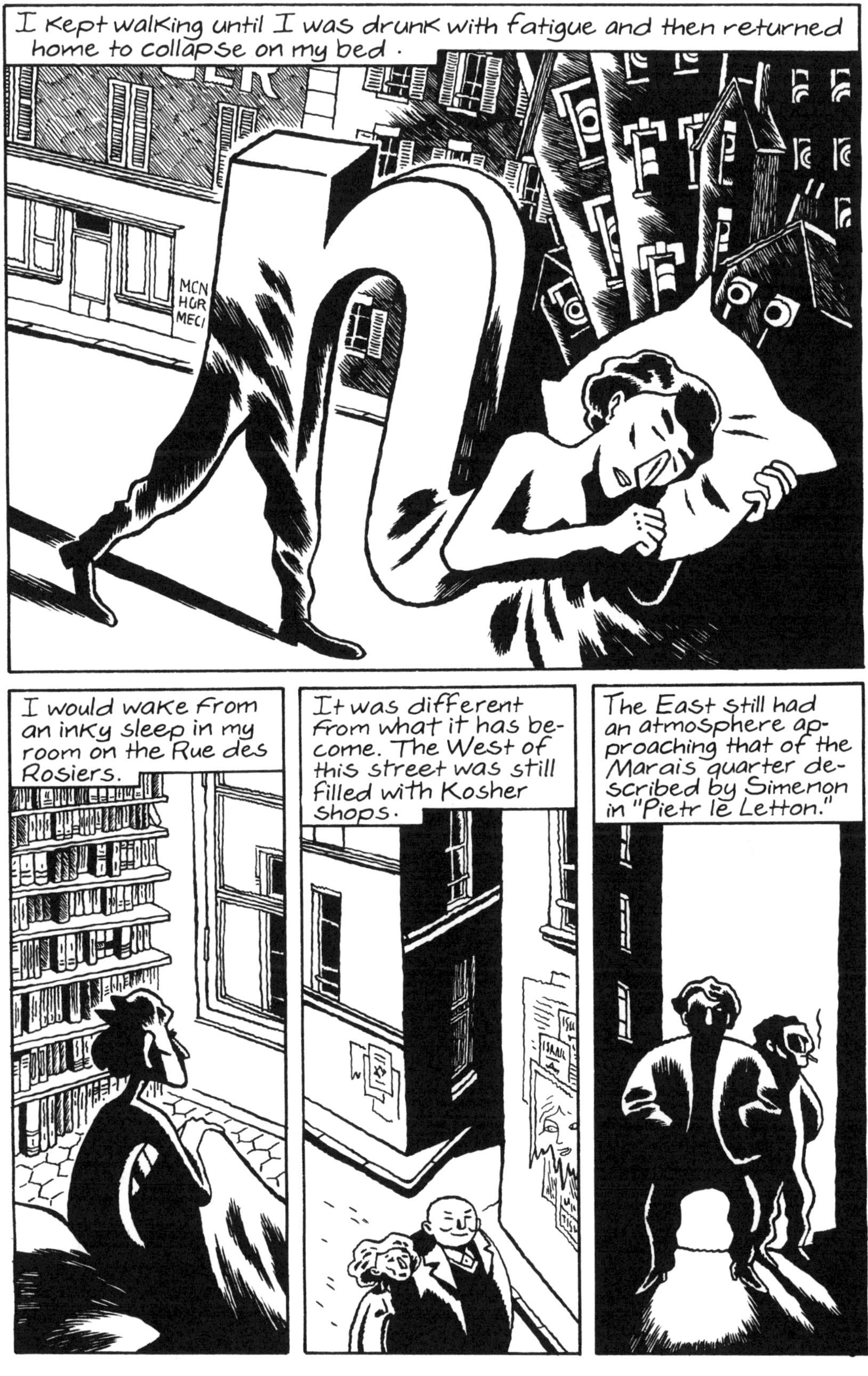
I kept walking until I was drunk with fatigue and then returned home to collapse on my bed.
I would wake from an inky sleep in my room on the Rue des Rosiers.
It was different from what it has become. The West of this street was still filled with Kosher shops.
The East still had an atmosphere approaching that of the Marais quarter described by Simenon in "Pietr le Letton."

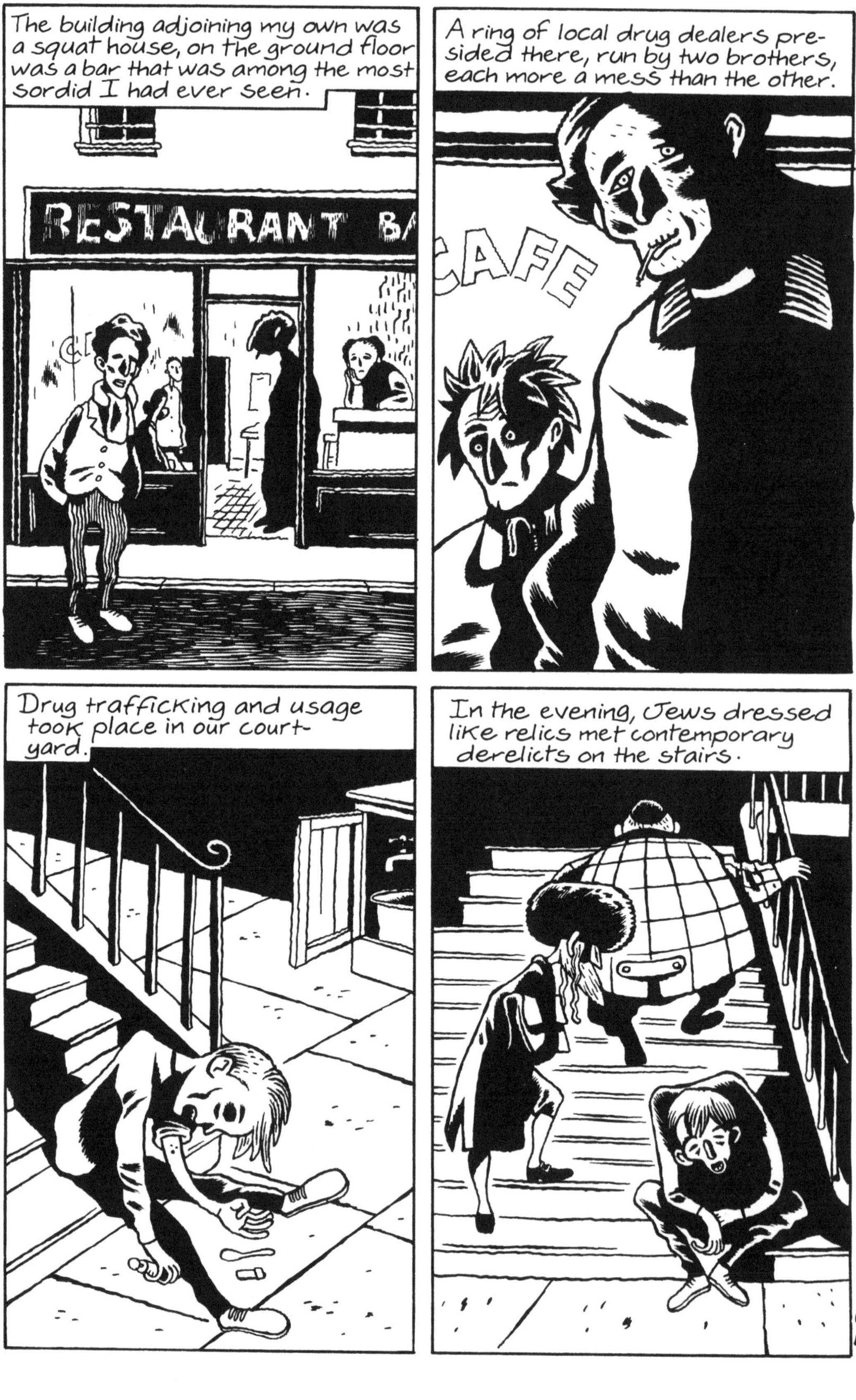
The building adjoining my own was a squat house, on the ground floor was a bar that was among the most sordid I had ever seen.
RESTAURANT BA
A ring of local drug dealers presided there, run by two brothers, each more a mess than the other.
CAFE
Drug trafficking and usage took place in our courtyard.
In the evening, Jews dressed like relics met contemporary derelicts on the stairs.

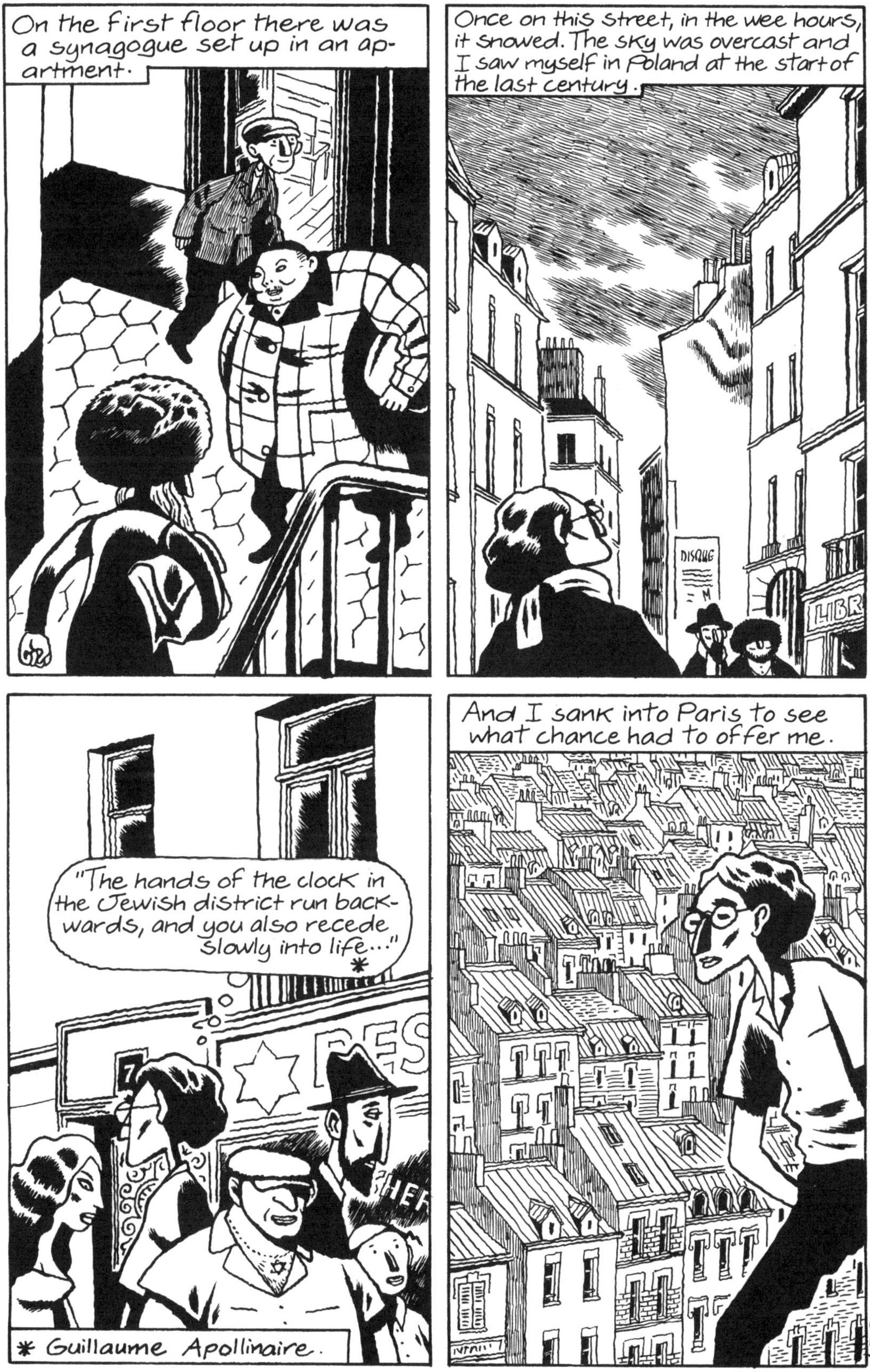
On the first floor there was a synagogue set up in an apartment.
Once on this street, in the wee hours, it snowed. The sky was overcast and I saw myself in Poland at the start of the last century.
DISQUE
LIBR
"The hands of the clock in the Jewish district run backwards, and you also recede slowly into life..." *
7
* Guillaume Apollinaire.
And I sank into Paris to see what chance had to offer me.

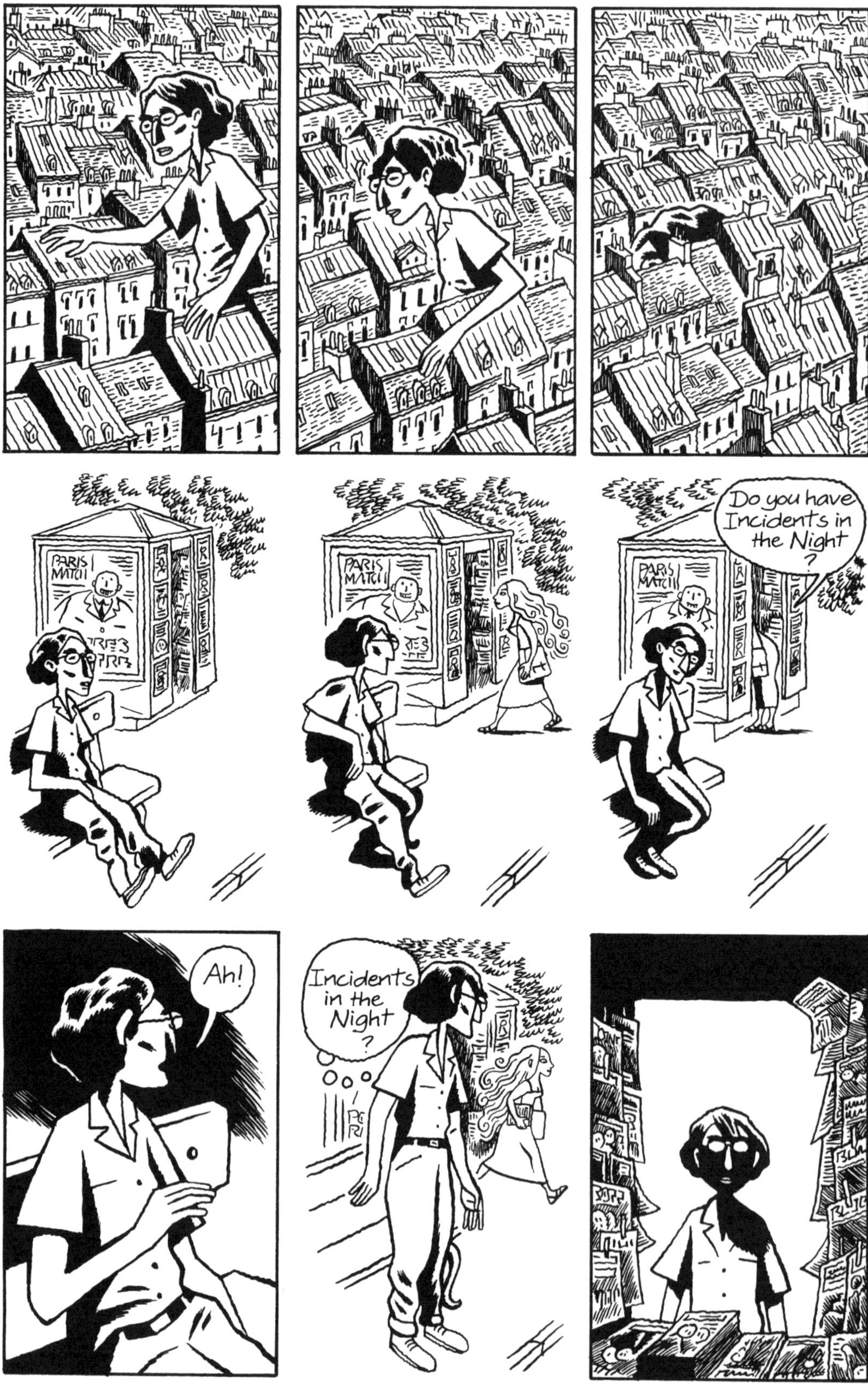
PARIS MATCH
Do you have Incidents in the Night ?
Ah!
Incidents in the Night ?

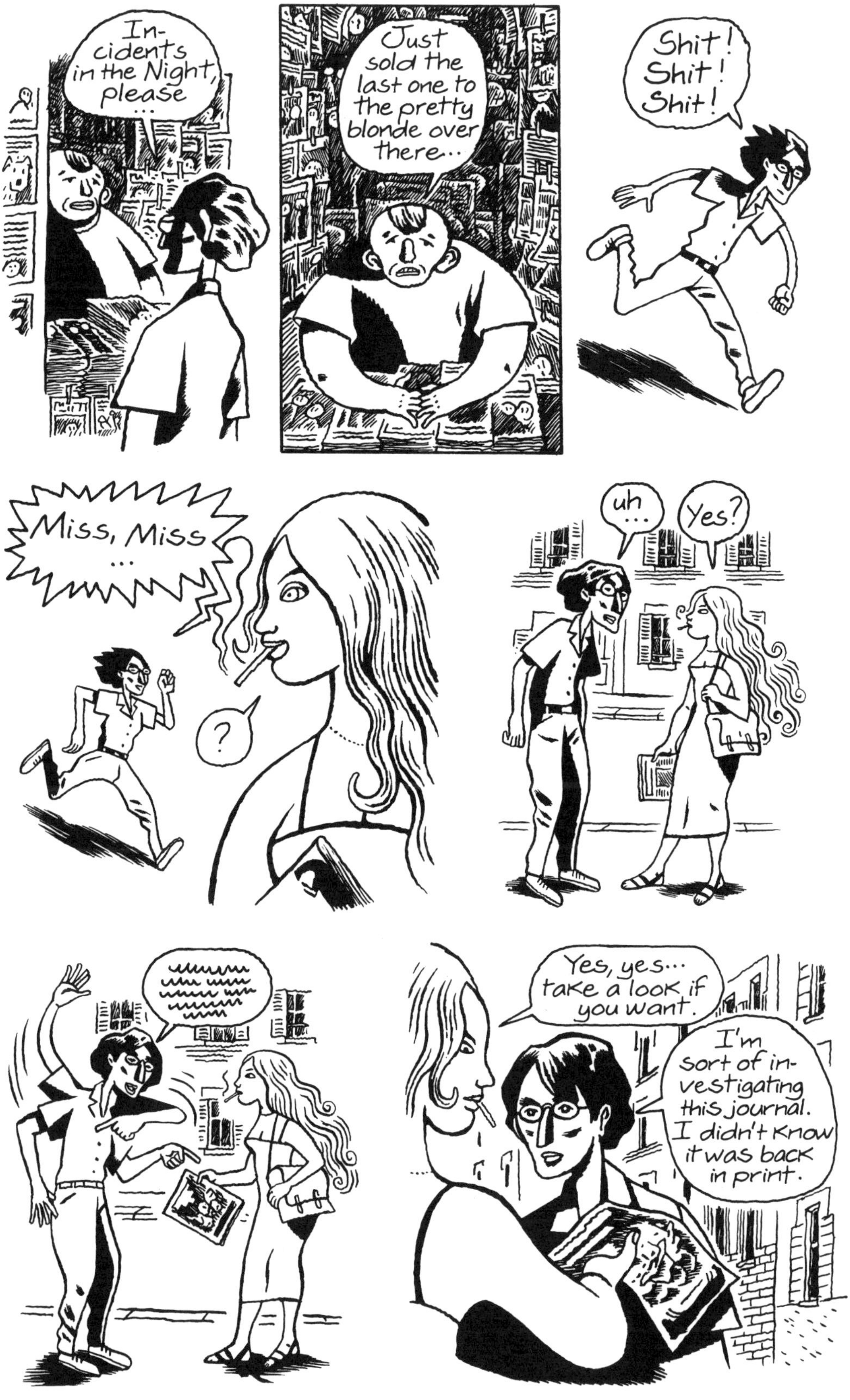
In-cidents in the Night, please ...
Just sold the last one to the pretty blonde over there...
Shit! Shit! Shit!
Miss, Miss ...
?
uh ...
Yes?
Yes, yes... take a look if you want.
I'm sort of in-vestigating this journal. I didn't know it was back in print.

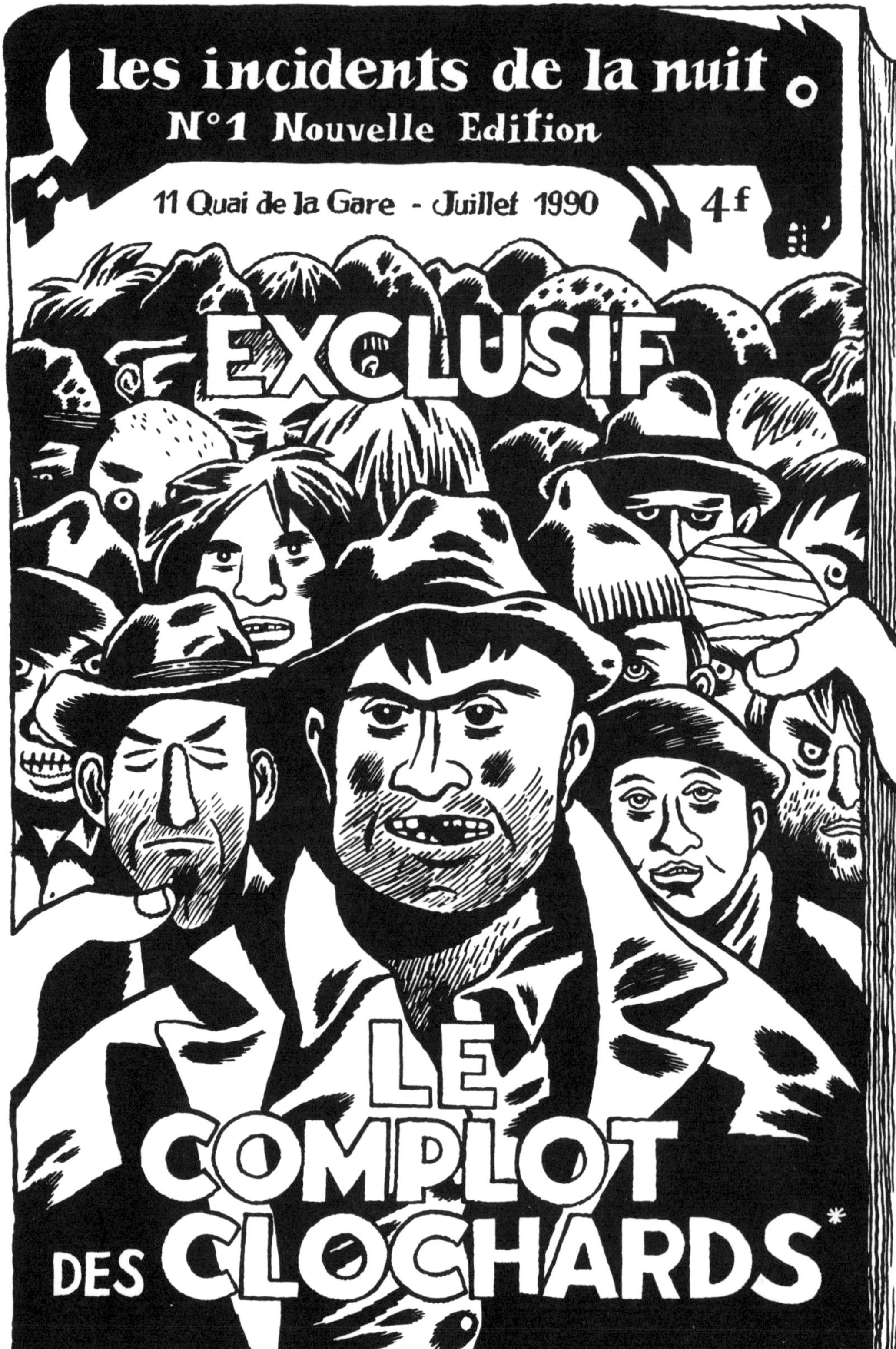
les incidents de la nuit
N°1 Nouvelle Edition
11 Quai de la Gare - Juillet 1990
4f
EXCLUSIF
LE COMPLOT DES CLOCHARDS*

* Exclusive, The Conspiracy of the Beggars

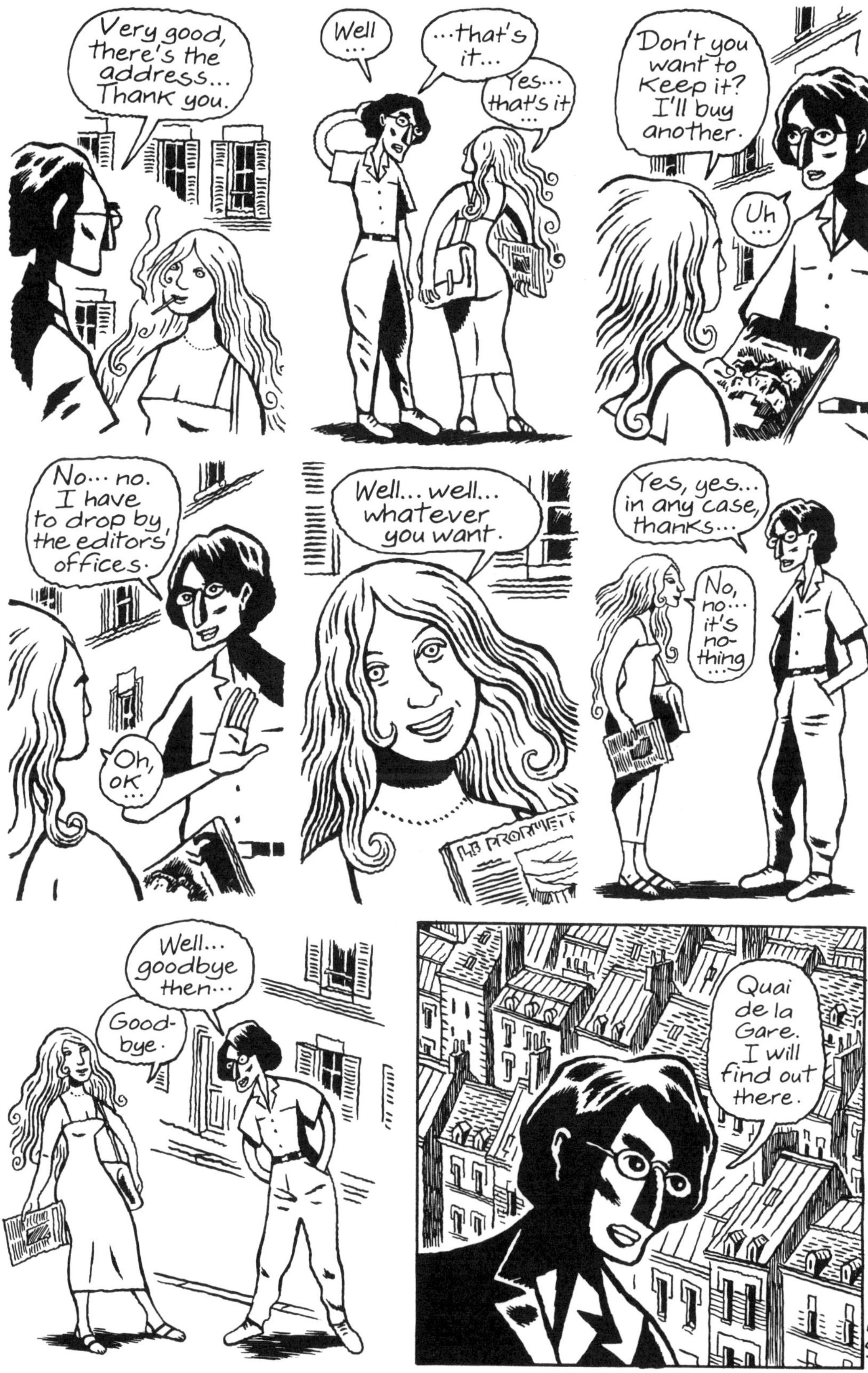
Very good, there's the address... Thank you.
Well ...
...that's it...
Yes... that's it ...
Don't you want to keep it? I'll buy another.
Uh ...
No... no. I have to drop by the editors' offices.
Oh, ok ...
Well... well... whatever you want.
Yes, yes... in any case, thanks...
No, no... it's nothing ...
Well... goodbye then...
Goodbye.
Quai de la Gare. I will find out there.

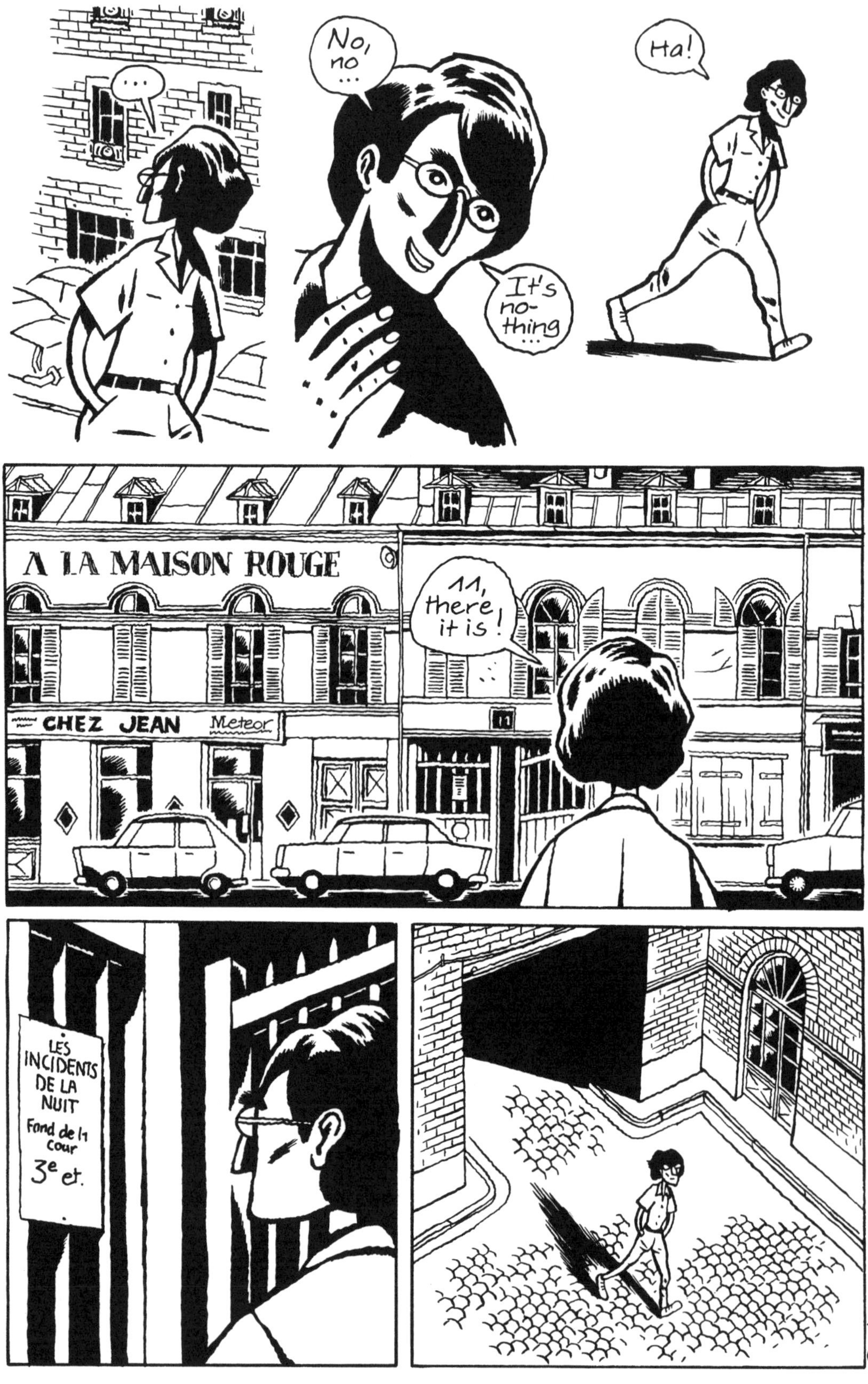
...
No, no ...
It's no-thing ...
Ha!
A LA MAISON ROUGE
CHEZ JEAN
Meteor
11, there it is!
11
LES INCIDENTS DE LA NUIT
Fond de la cour
3e et.

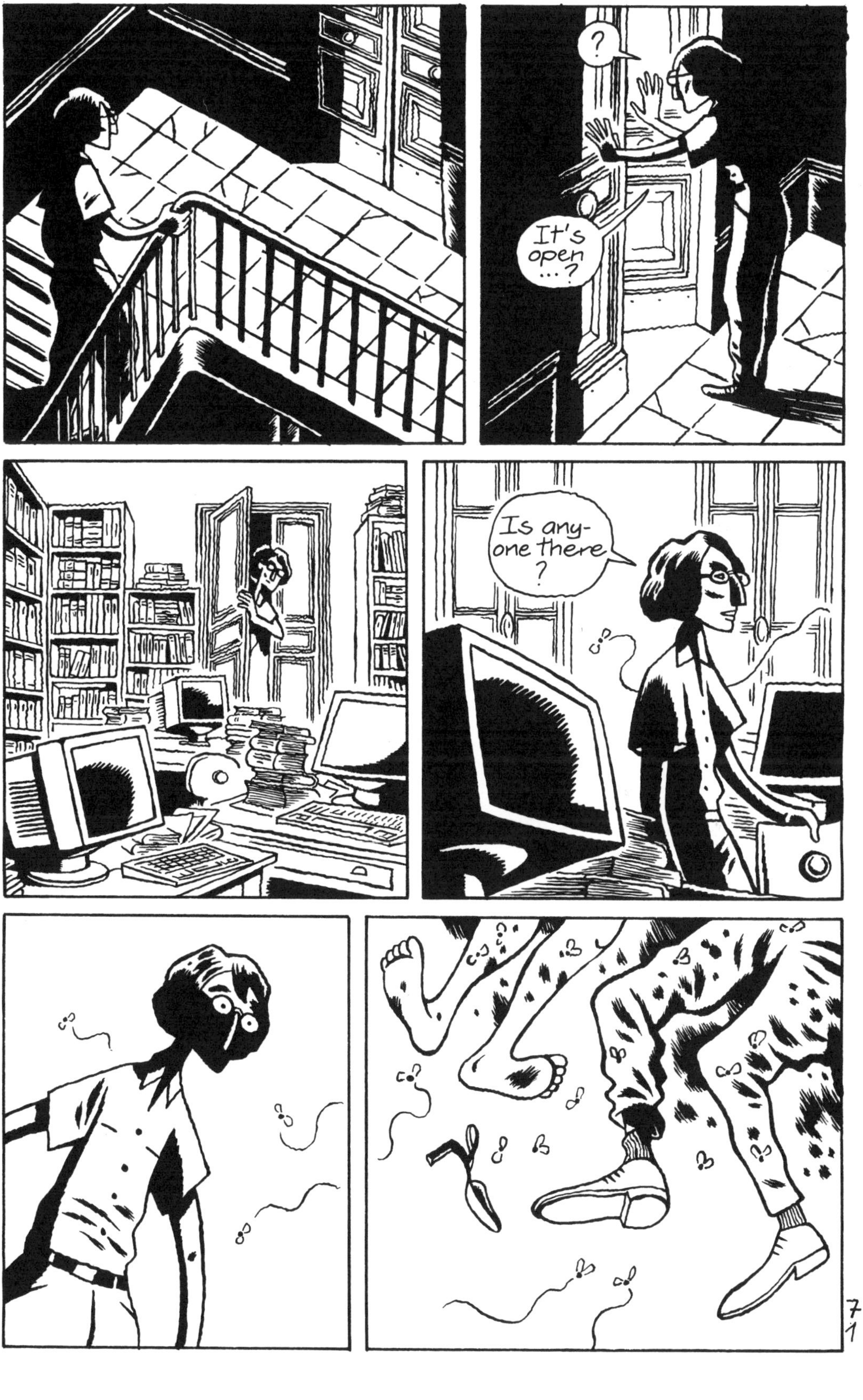
?
It's open ...?
Is any-one there ?

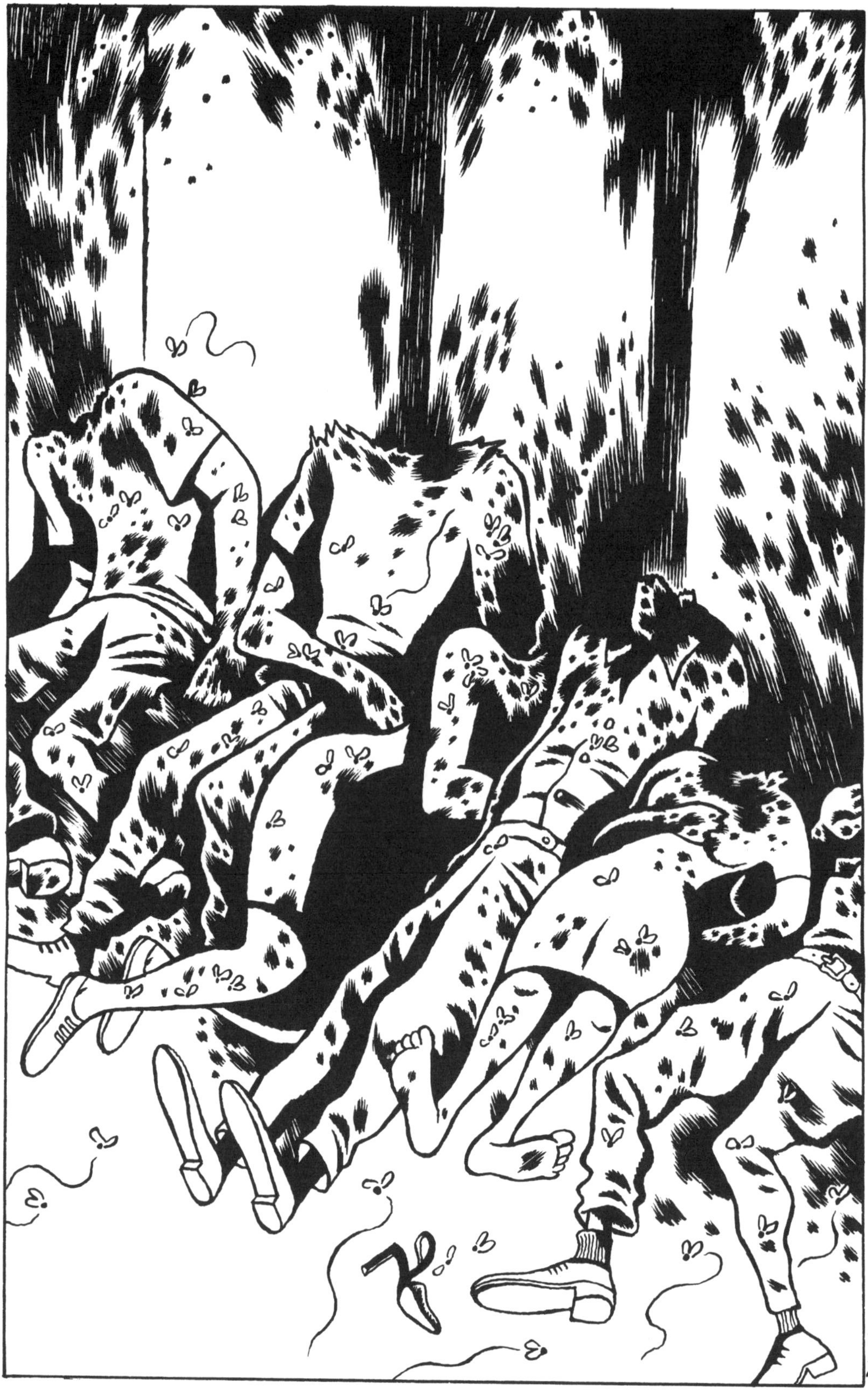

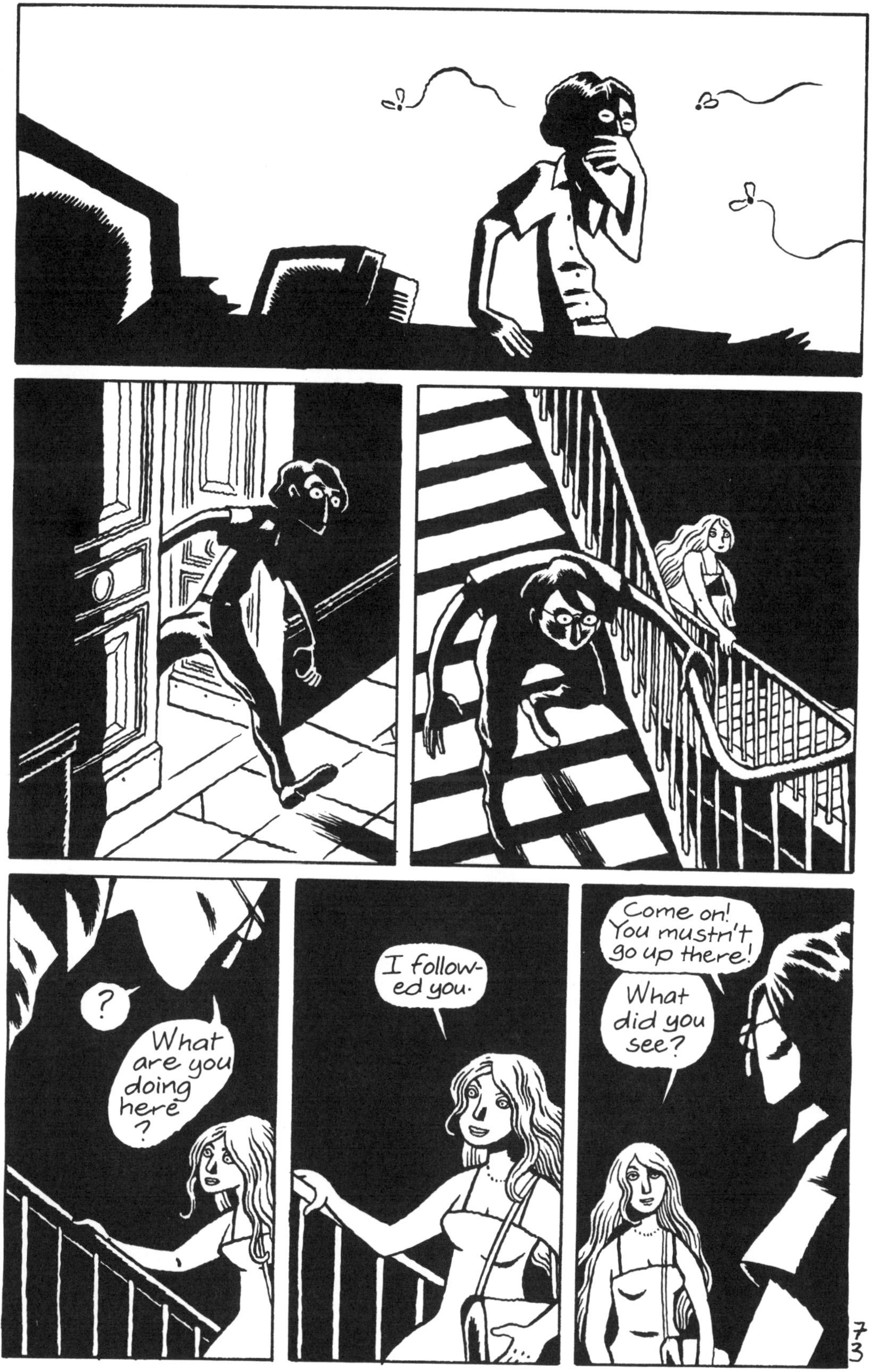
?
What are you doing here?
I follow-ed you.
Come on! You mustn't go up there!
What did you see?

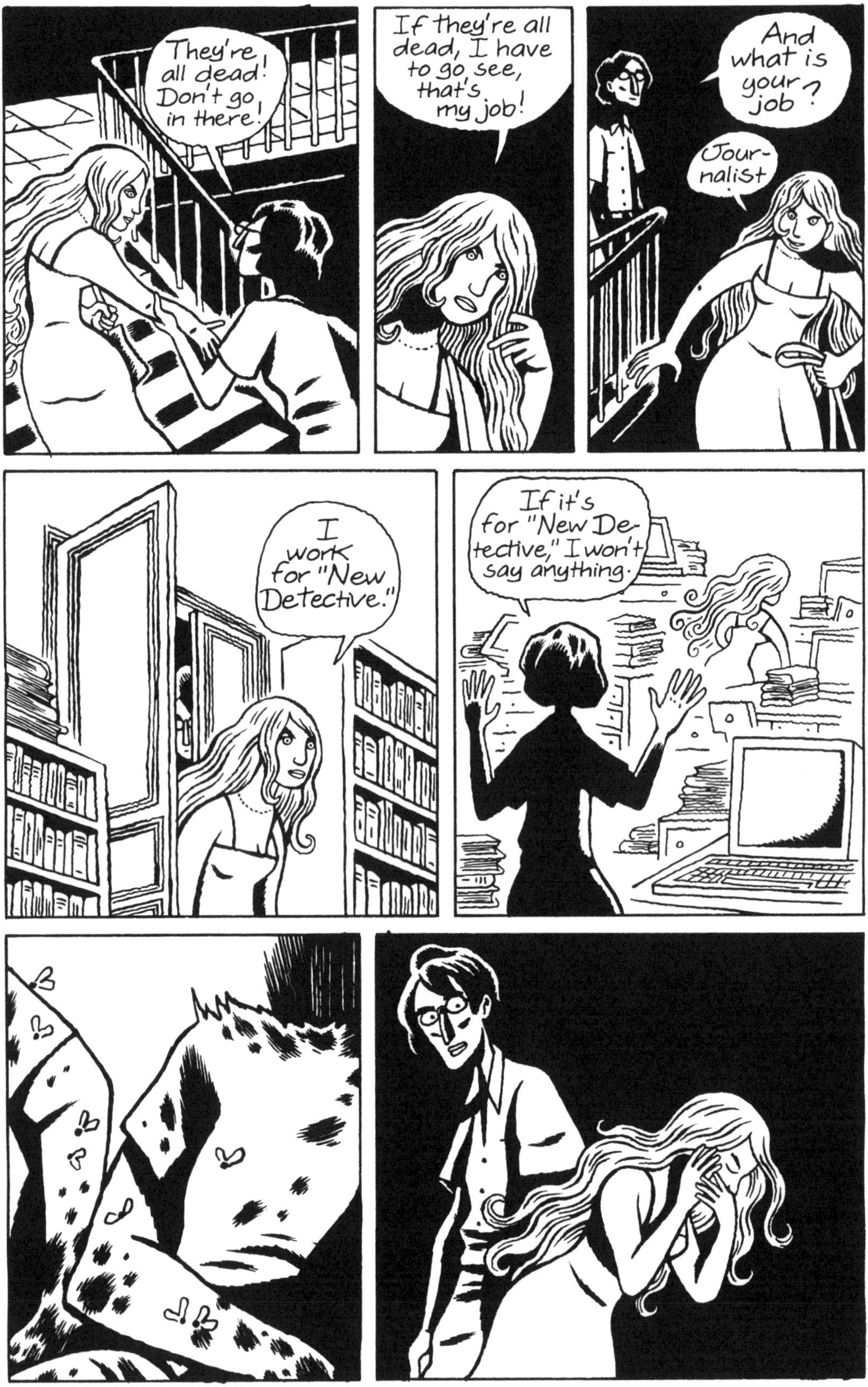
They're all dead! Don't go in there!
If they're all dead, I have to go see, that's my job!
And what is your job?
Jour-nalist
I work for "New Detective."
If it's for "New De-tective," I won't say anything.

I'm going to speak about all this with Commissioner Hunborgne...

You know? Hunborgne?

Yes yes...

Hunborgne! I had met him several years before.

The owner of the fourth floor apartment wanted to evict his tenants, who I knew.

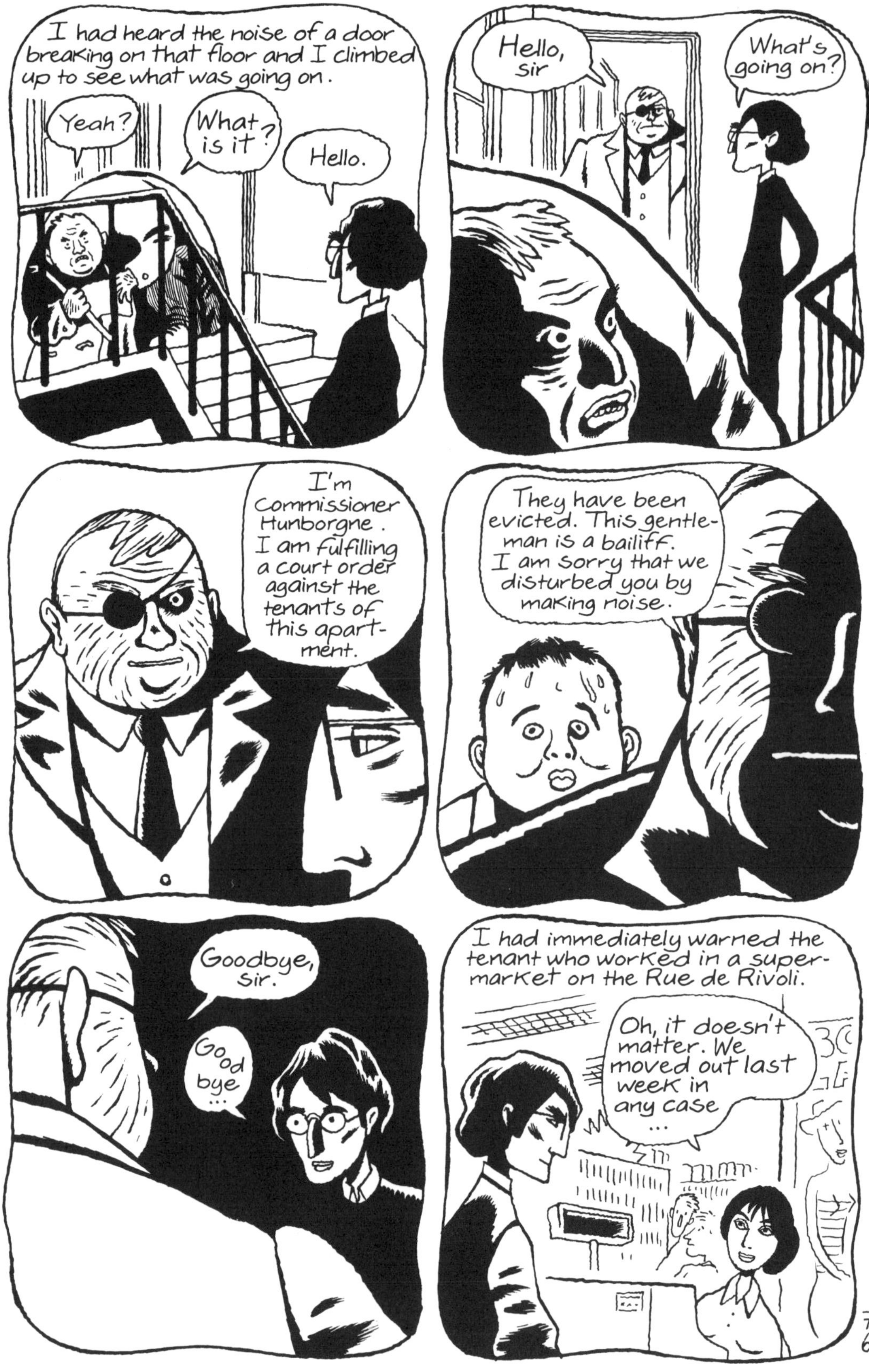
I had heard the noise of a door breaking on that floor and I climbed up to see what was going on.
Yeah?
What is it?
Hello.
Hello, sir
What's going on?
I'm Commissioner Hunborgne. I am fulfilling a court order against the tenants of this apartment.
They have been evicted. This gentleman is a bailiff. I am sorry that we disturbed you by making noise.
Goodbye, sir.
Goodbye...
I had immediately warned the tenant who worked in a supermarket on the Rue de Rivoli.
Oh, it doesn't matter. We moved out last week in any case...

I thought again of this trio while descending the stairs. The obese locksmith, suprised while doing a dirty job, was rude.

The bailiff was in a cold sweat.

The commissioner fulfilled his role with neither fear nor agressiveness, but with dignity.

Later, our paths crossed again.

A crowd in front of a cafe had attracted my gaze.

E D'OR

A settling of scores?

The other dashed right off!

He was fired upon!

He's losing blood!

77

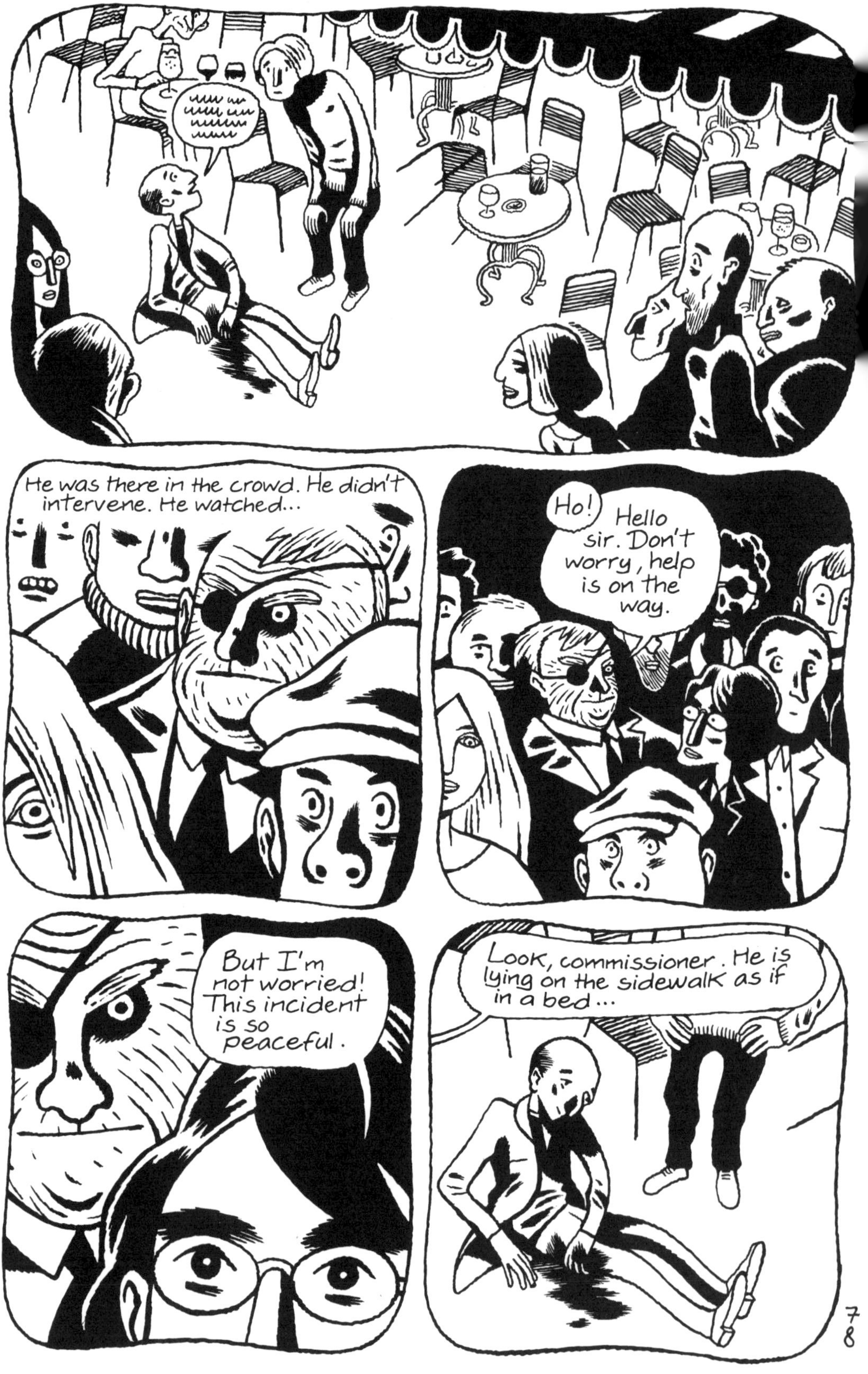
He was there in the crowd. He didn't intervene. He watched...
Ho!
Hello sir. Don't worry, help is on the way.
But I'm not worried! This incident is so peaceful.
Look, commissioner. He is lying on the sidewalk as if in a bed...

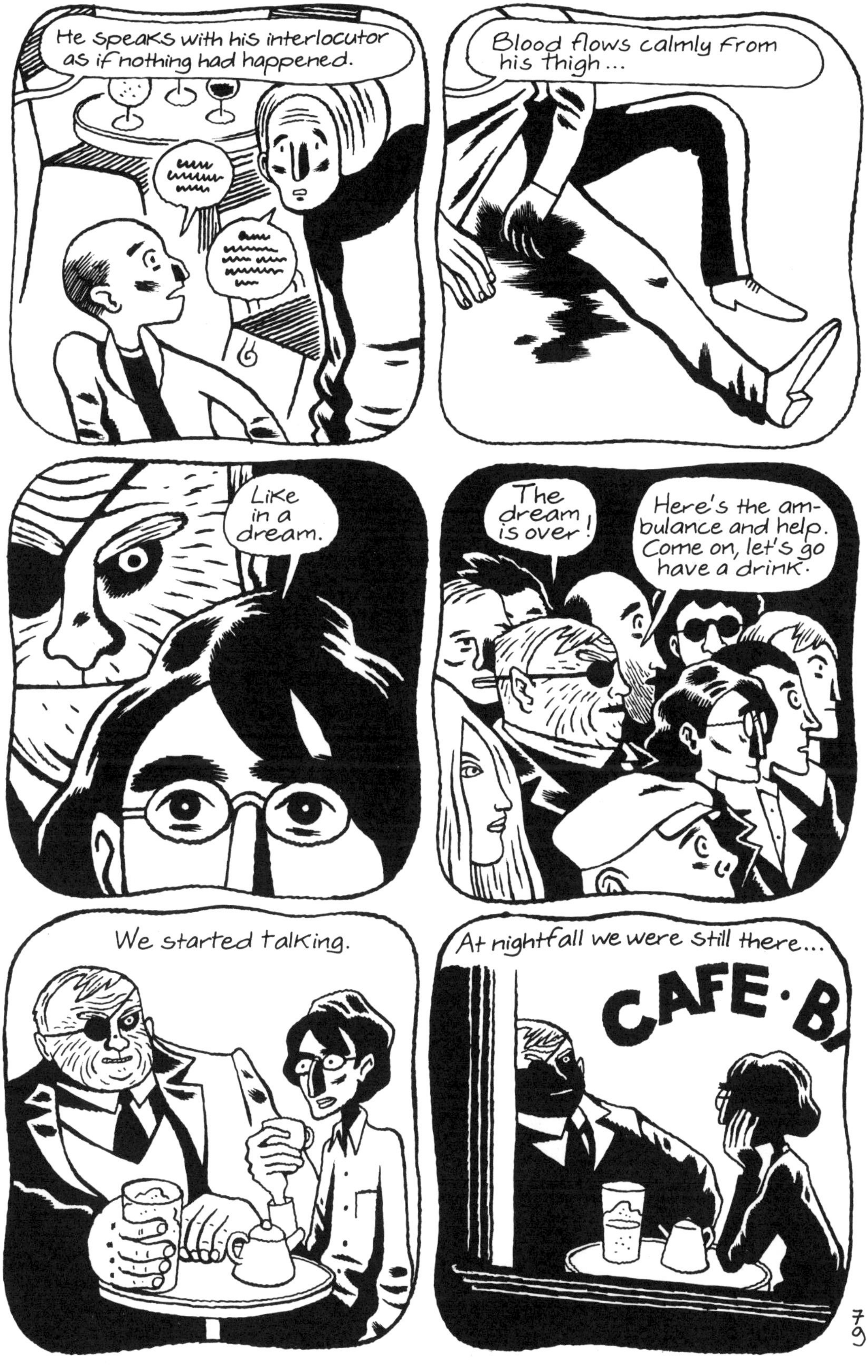
He speaks with his interlocutor as if nothing had happened.
Blood flows calmly from his thigh...
Like in a dream.
The dream is over!
Here's the ambulance and help. Come on, let's go have a drink.
We started talking.
At nightfall we were still there...
CAFE · B

He had participated in all the under-ground movements of the 4th and 5th Republic.

The fight against the MNA and the NLF during the Algerian War. *

The tracking down of partisans of the OAS at the end of the same war.

A bomb placed at the door of his domicile had disfigured him.

In the 1970s he investigated members of the French Connection, the Lyonnais Gang, or the Zemmour brothers.

But he also investi-gated movements of the far left and the far right.

* MNA: **National Algerian Movement**. FLN: National Liberation Front. These two factions of freedom fighters had a bloody war.

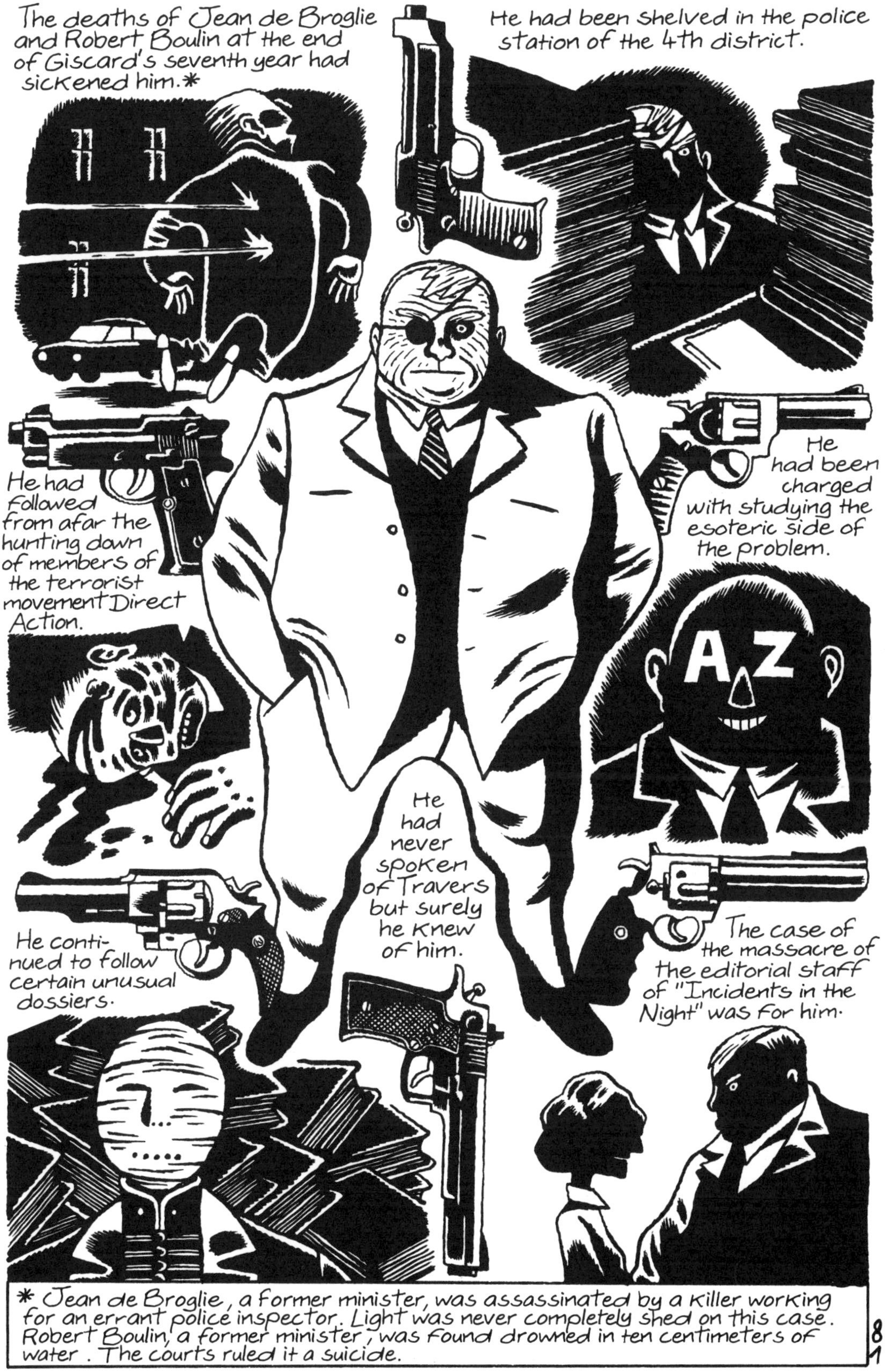
The deaths of Jean de Broglie and Robert Boulin at the end of Giscard's seventh year had sickened him.*
He had been shelved in the police station of the 4th district.
He had followed from afar the hunting down of members of the terrorist movement Direct Action.
He had been charged with studying the esoteric side of the problem.
A Z
He had never spoken of Travers but surely he knew of him.
He continued to follow certain unusual dossiers.
The case of the massacre of the editorial staff of "Incidents in the Night" was for him.

* Jean de Broglie, a former minister, was assassinated by a killer working for an errant police inspector. Light was never completely shed on this case. Robert Boulin, a former minister, was found drowned in ten centimeters of water. The courts ruled it a suicide.

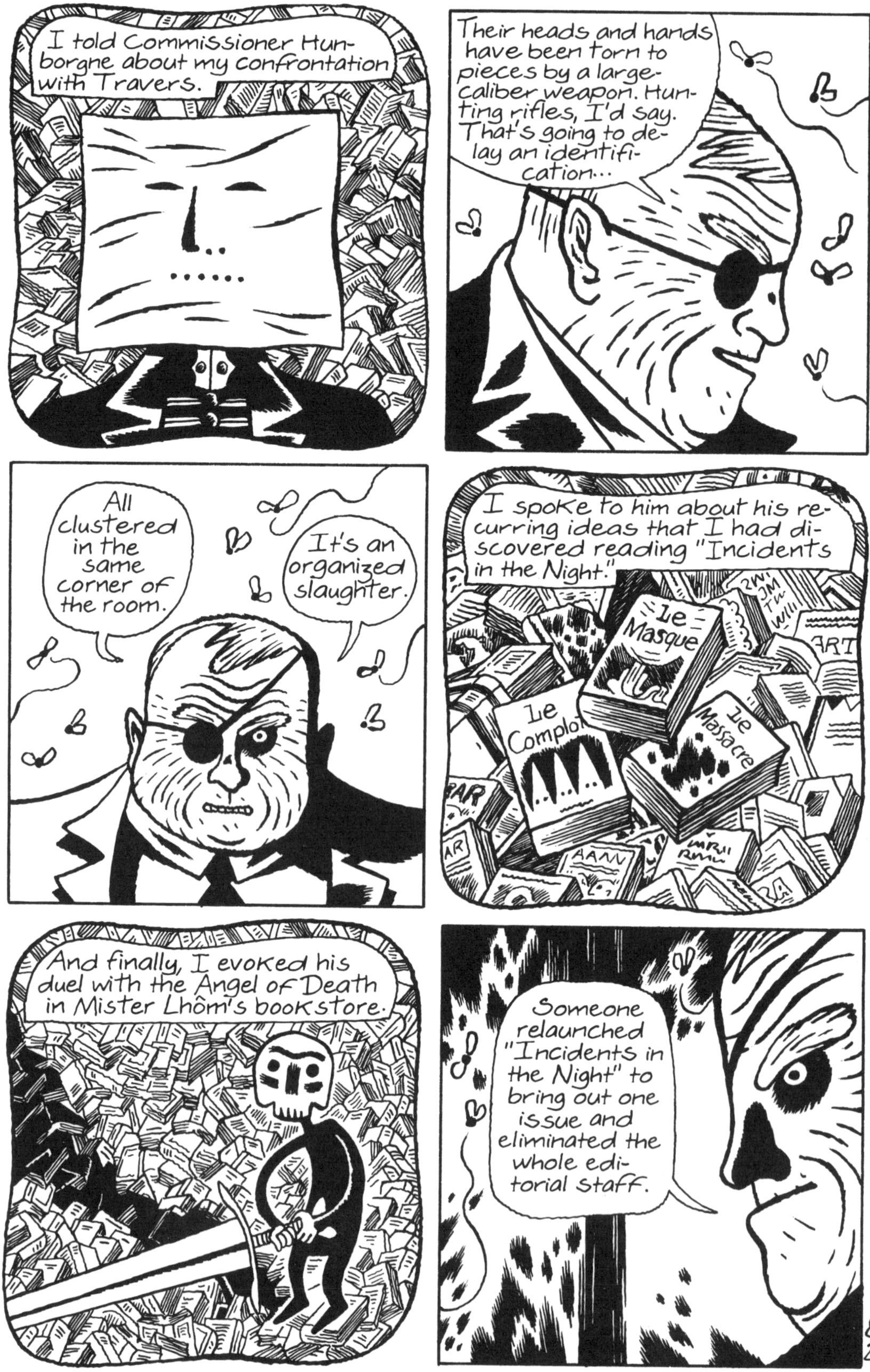
I told Commissioner Hunborgne about my confrontation with Travers.
Their heads and hands have been torn to pieces by a large-caliber weapon. Hunting rifles, I'd say. That's going to delay an identification...
All clustered in the same corner of the room.
It's an organized slaughter.
I spoke to him about his recurring ideas that I had discovered reading "Incidents in the Night."
Le Masque
Le Complot
Le Massacre
ART
And finally, I evoked his duel with the Angel of Death in Mister Lhôm's bookstore.
Someone relaunched "Incidents in the Night" to bring out one issue and eliminated the whole editorial staff.

But he's dead! I saw blood at the bottom of the bucket!

It was a mytho-logical death. He needed to die to be reborn.

It's Travers!

He's still alive!

He needs extra time to accomplish his mission. His first task was to obtain a little bit of extra life.

There he starts his mission as such by putting out a new issue of "Incidents."

And by then slaugh-tering the editorial staff, he places himself again under the pro-tection of the god Enn. The slaughter is an offering.

8
3

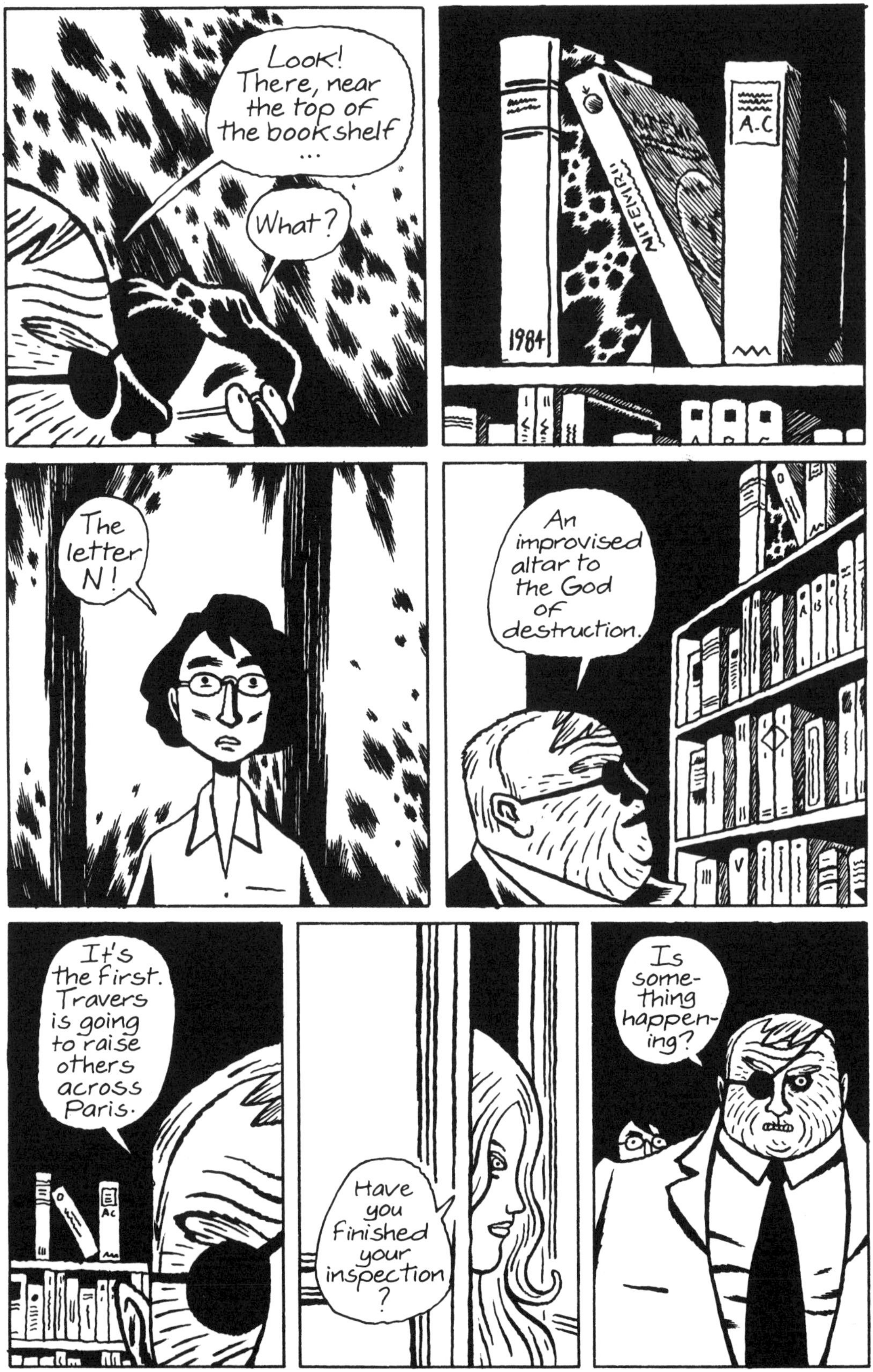
Look! There, near the top of the bookshelf ...
What?
1984
NITEMIR!!
A.C
The letter N!
An improvised altar to the God of destruction.
It's the first. Travers is going to raise others across Paris.
Have you finished your inspection ?
Is some-thing happen-ing?

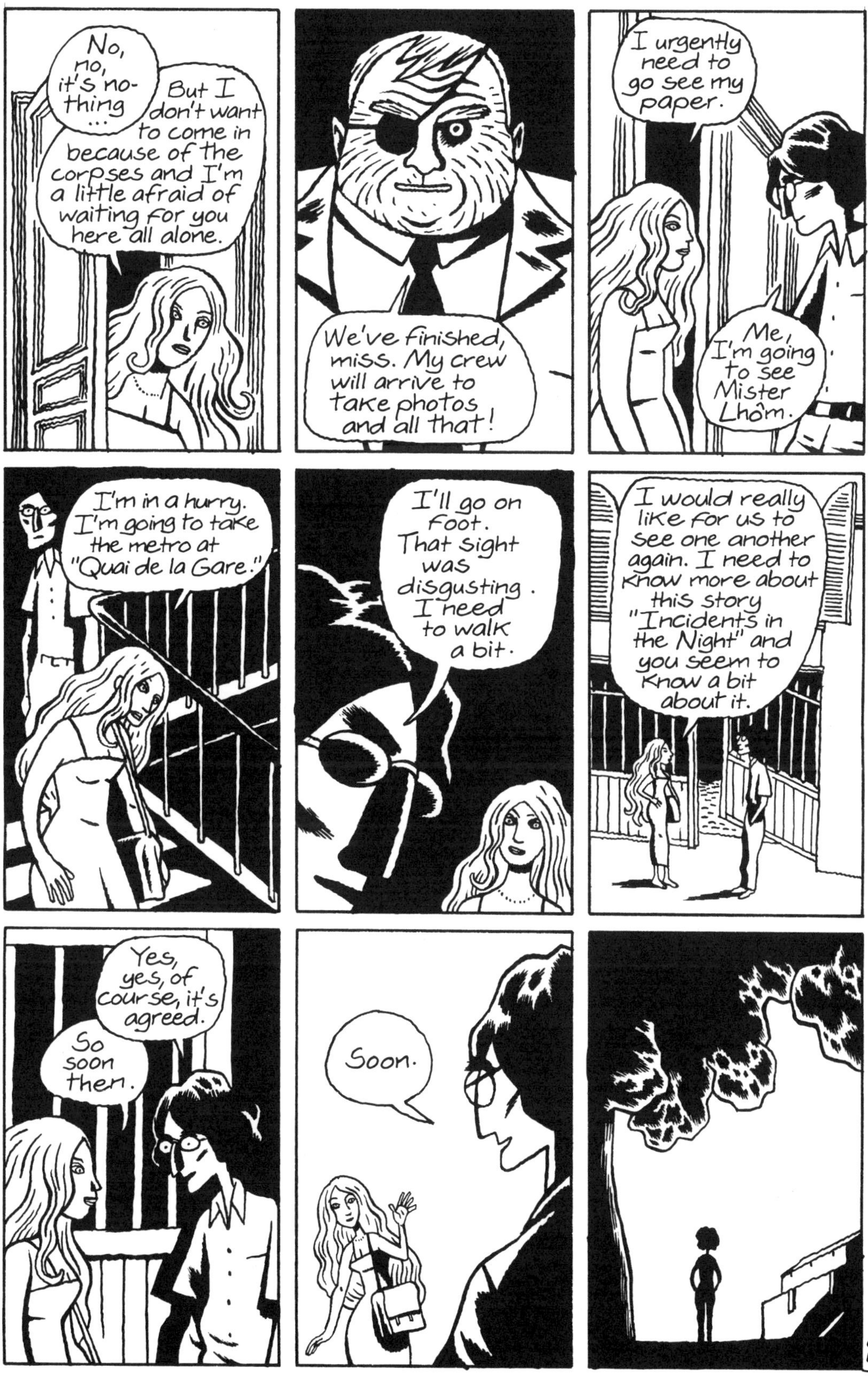
No, no, it's nothing...
But I don't want to come in because of the corpses and I'm a little afraid of waiting for you here all alone.
We've finished, miss. My crew will arrive to take photos and all that!
I urgently need to go see my paper.
Me, I'm going to see Mister Lhôm.
I'm in a hurry. I'm going to take the metro at "Quai de la Gare."
I'll go on foot. That sight was disgusting. I need to walk a bit.
I would really like for us to see one another again. I need to know more about this story "Incidents in the Night" and you seem to know a bit about it.
Yes, yes, of course, it's agreed.
So soon then.
Soon.

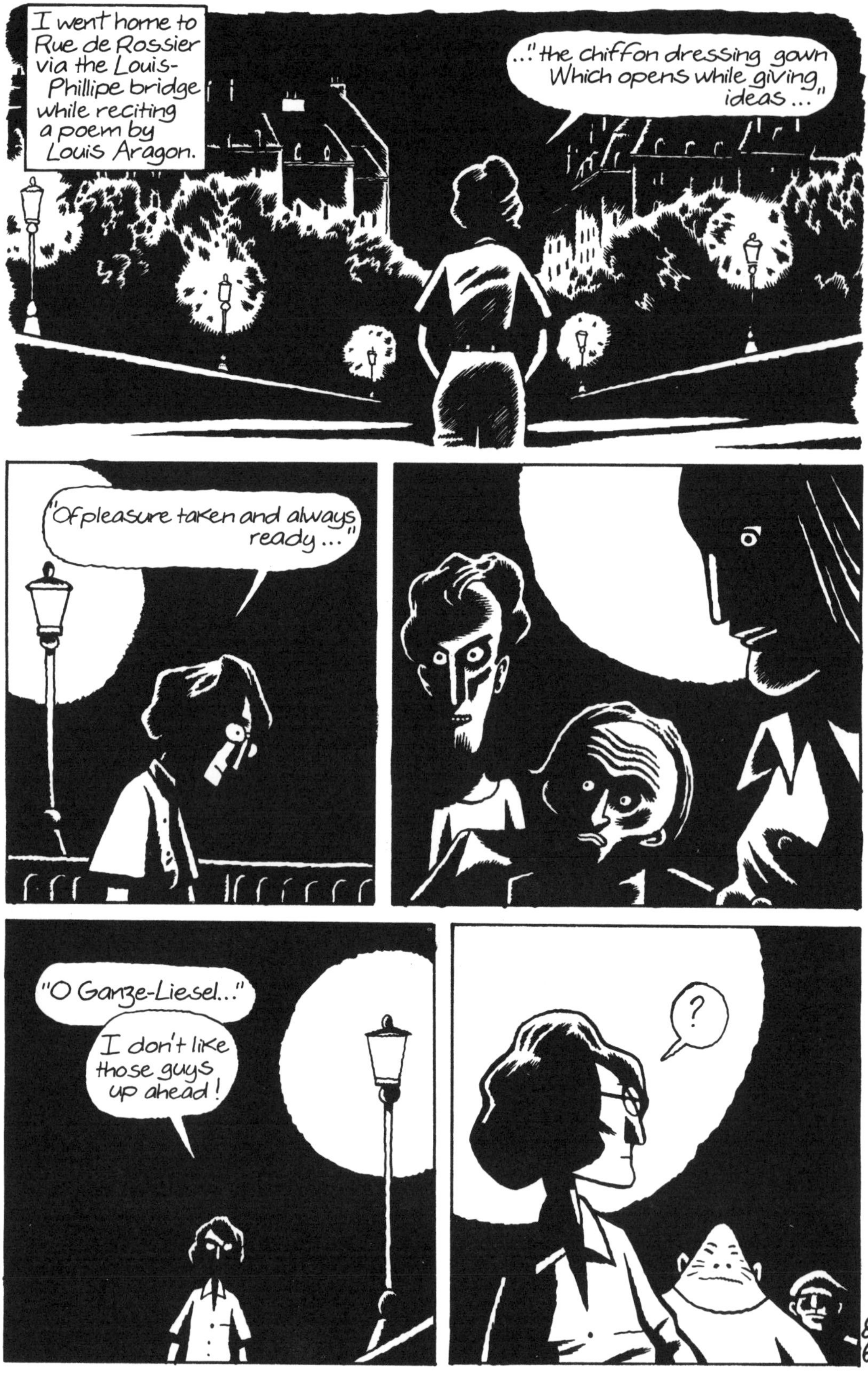
I went home to Rue de Rossier via the Louis-Phillipe bridge while reciting a poem by Louis Aragon.
..." the chiffon dressing gown Which opens while giving ideas ..."
"Of pleasure taken and always ready ..."
"O Ganze-Liesel..."
I don't like those guys up ahead!
?

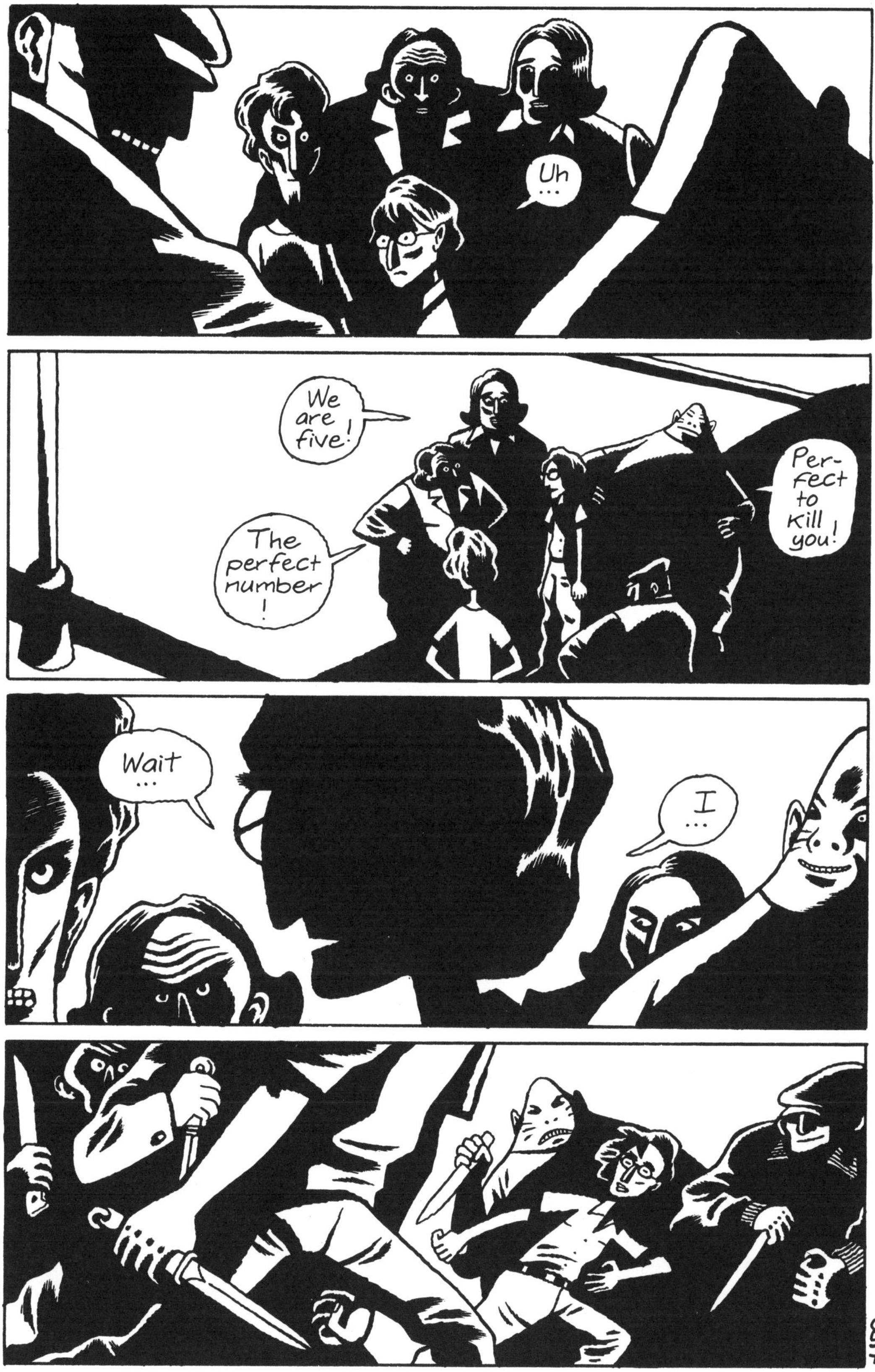
Uh ...
We are five!
The perfect number !
Per-fect to kill you!
Wait ...
I ...

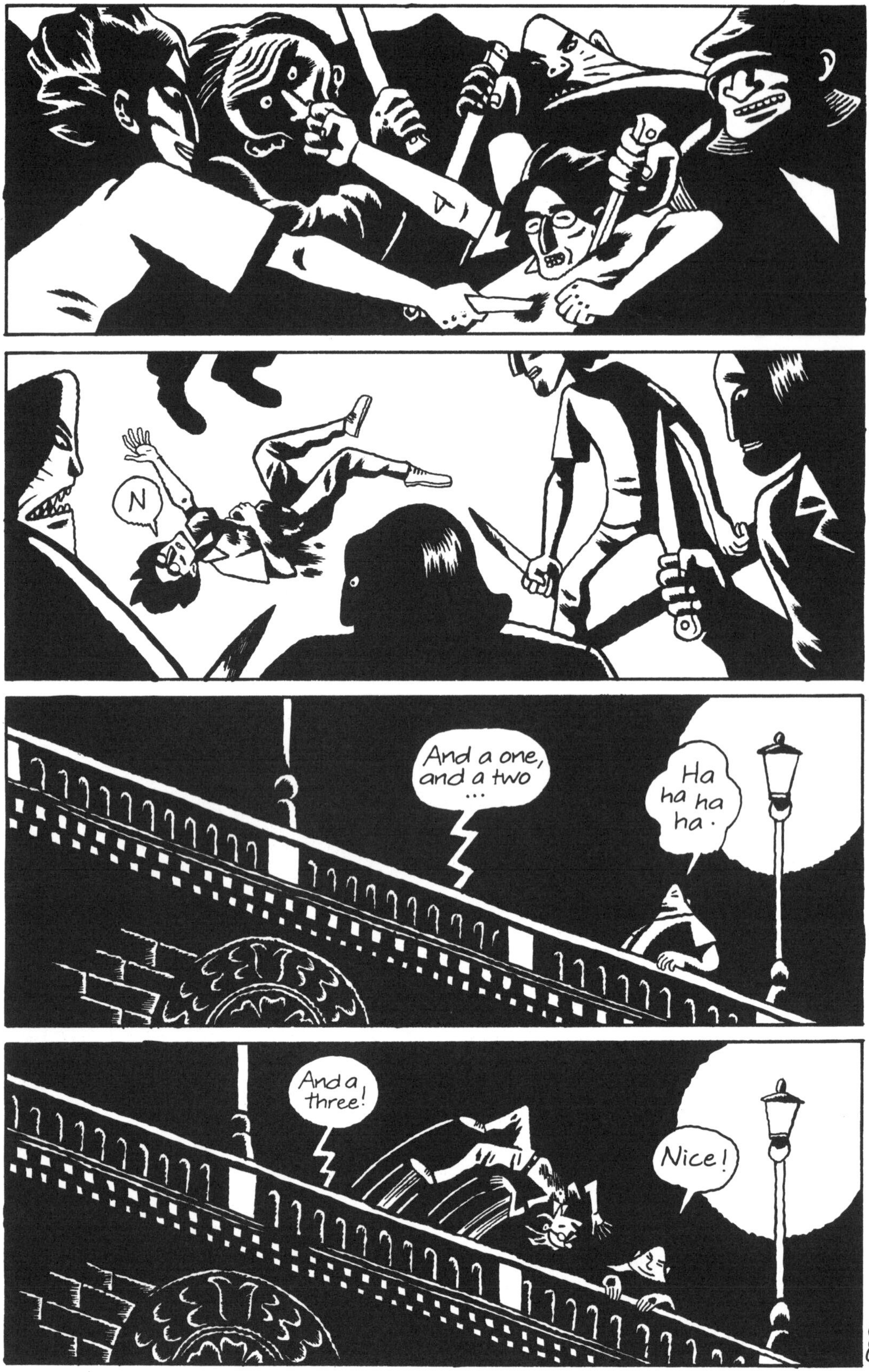
N
And a one, and a two ...
Ha ha ha ha.
And a three!
Nice!

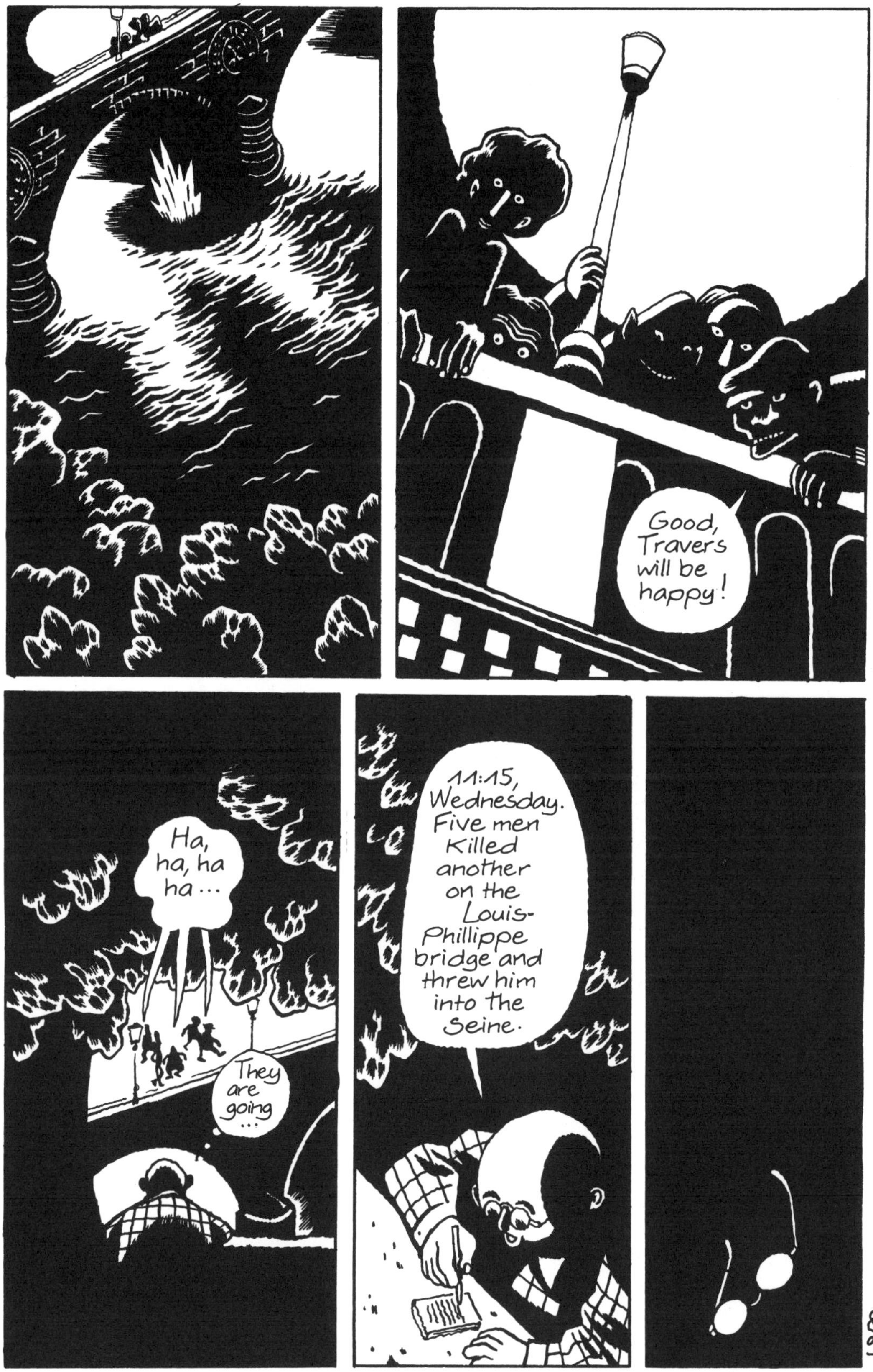
Good, Travers will be happy!
Ha, ha, ha ha...
They are going...
11:15, Wednesday. Five men Killed another on the Louis-Phillippe bridge and threw him into the Seine.

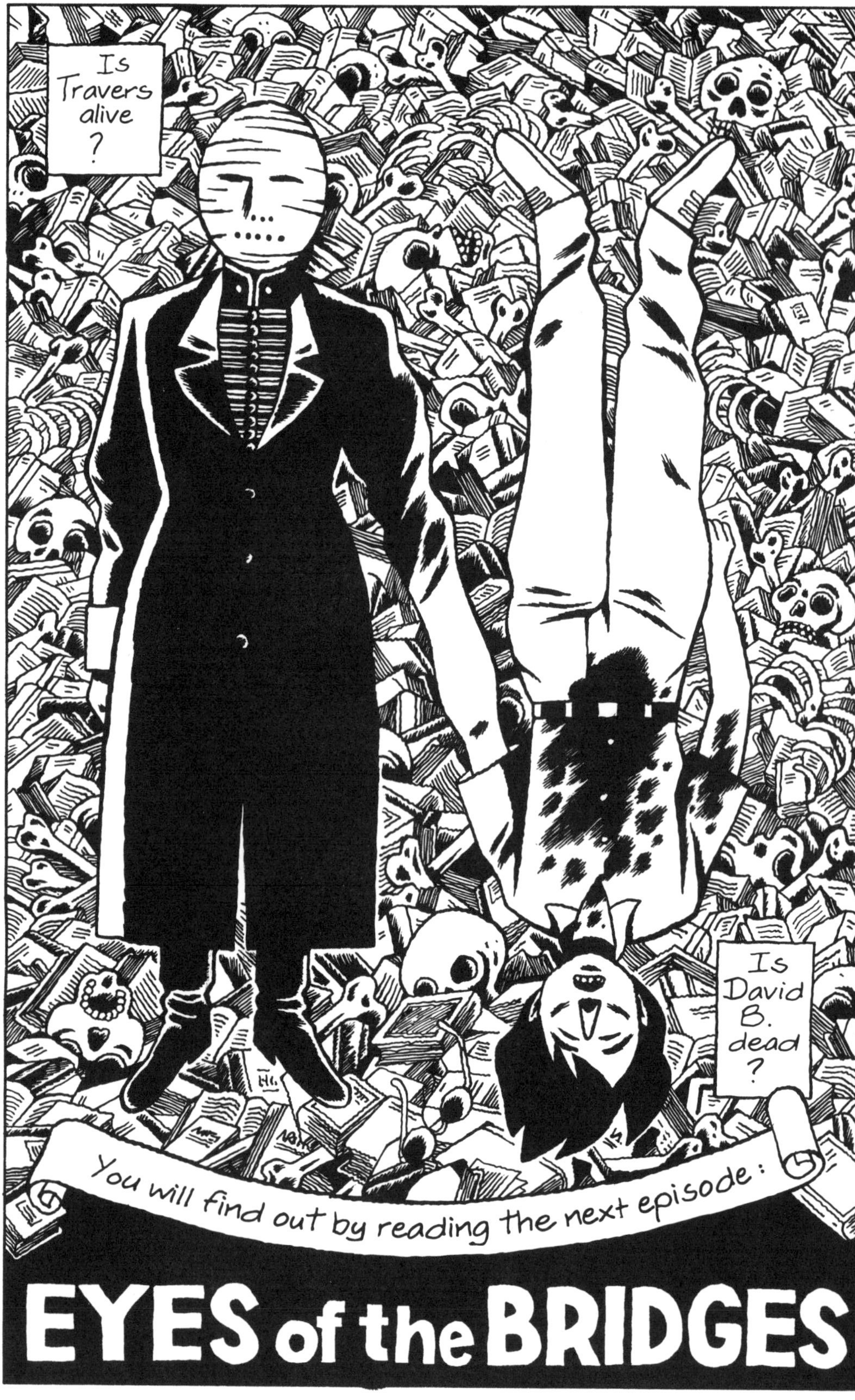
Is Travers alive ?
Is David B. dead ?
You will find out by reading the next episode :
EYES of the BRIDGES

Afterword

by Brian Evenson

A third of the way through David B.'s *Incidents in the Night*, an eccentric editor named Emile Travers, who sports a book in the place of his head, leaps "into a letter like into a lake and took its form, thus escaping the Angel of Death." Travers has dodged the Angel of Death six times by hiding within books, masquerading within language. If he can escape a seventh, he tells the character David B., then he will become immortal. He is seeking David B.'s help because he is "certain that you've found the way to shake off Death by way of a book!"

David B., the fictional David B. and not the author—or perhaps both the fictional and the real David B., for there is rarely as clean a separation between the real and the imagined as we might like to think—is intrigued by this. If he is able to hide Travers a seventh and final time, maybe it will be possible to escape death himself.

He hides Travers within a book called *The Desert*, the pages of which are covered with row upon row of the letter N. With the letter N representing "Enn", the unknown god of the Greeks, the god of emptiness, of the void, each letter of the book becomes a sort of chasm. David B. believes that the Angel of Death will get lost among all these chasms, and be unable to find Travers in time to kill him at the appointed hour.

And indeed, with time having expired, it is Travers who clambers out of the book rather than Azraël, the Angel of Death. David B. thinks Travers has won, that he's found a way to defeat Death. But quickly he comes to understand that the figure who has climbed out of the book may not be Travers at all, but the Angel of Death wearing Travers' face like a mask. Travers seems to be dead.

Whether this death is definitive or reversible is the subject of the rest of the first volume of *Incidents in the Night*. The word "travers" means "across" or "through" in French, and even after the editor's death David B. keeps uncovering traces of Travers that make him suspect that Travers might either still be alive, or be capable of being brought back to life.

I have not been able to determine whether *The Desert* is a real book or an imaginary one: with David B., it could be either. The idea of a book that is the repetition of a single letter, over and over again, seems the opposite of the library found in Jorge Luis Borges' Library of Babel. It is a kind of ritualized and monotonous repetition that opens up into emptiness. But, then again, with Borges' library containing all possible books, both written and unwritten, and stretching on seemingly forever, *The Desert* would be part of it. Just one book among many that you might get lost in, in a library that you can't help but lose yourself in as well.

It's no coincidence that a used bookshop becomes the site for the battle with Death in *Incidents in the Night*. Rendered in David B's moody and inimitable style it takes on a symbolic resonance that it's hard not to wish all bookstores had. Travers slips into *The Desert* and Azraël must find him. He finds and enters the book almost immediately, leaving David B. and the bookshop owner to listen to the blows of Azraël's sword as they resound from within the pages. "There have been so many duels with Death here," Lhôm, the bookshop owner, tells David B. "Not one of them has succeeded, you know."

And yet we keep trying. What makes books quintessentially what they are is the promise that hides in their pages. The sense that we can metaphorically—or even, with holy books, for "real"—escape death through them, as authors and as readers. Even if they don't believe that books will really save them from death, writers still hold tight to the belief of living on after our deaths if their books are still read. What we want ultimately as humans is not to be forgotten. Indeed, one of the best cases for fiction being experiential rather than a mimetic reproduction of the real, is this: we still think it can save us from something—from being forgotten, from oblivion, from death.

David B. understands that subconsciously we search books for magics that will help us avoid being confronted by our own mortality, and he has made this the conscious subject of *Incidents in the Night*. Other writers have done this, but few have done it so well. David B. does it both with words and images, and does it marvelously and with great impact. We will not find these magics—rationally we know this. But we might still find the promise of them, even as we see within them the reflection of our own future corpse.

The only way to keep the magic from dissipating is to stop short of death, even if just barely. This volume of Incidents of the Night ends without ending, with a doubly-articulated question. David B. and Travers lie side by side, head to foot, on a pile of books and bones, with the arm of the one blending into the arm of the other like an umbilical cord between them or like the band of flesh joining Siamese twins. "Is Travers alive?" the top of the page asks. "Is David B. dead?" the bottom asks. The uncertainty of the death of the one is mirrored in the uncertainty of the continued life of the other, and we are left in that wavery space where, at best, any answer is tentative, suspended. We'll have to wait for David B.'s second volume, almost two decades in coming, for whatever further answers it can offer.

That may be all that books can offer us: the ability to think that someone has escaped death in the brief moment before we begin to worry that we're mistaken, that maybe it's just that Death has stolen his face.

Appendix I

The book titles around the outside of page 4, beginning in the upper right hand corner and moving clockwise, are:

{ illegible }

Swastika [This is probably the book by Junichiro Tanizaki by the same title, but we can't tell for certain.]

Le Dernier Mandrin, Jean-Baptiste Buisson

{ illegible }

The Battle for the Atlantic [probably the one written by Commandant Pierre Weiss]

The Epic of Kings, Ferdowski

Ivan the Terrible, Henry Vallotton

The Assassins: a Radical Sect in Islam, Bernard Lewis, preface by Maxime Rodinson

The Golem, Gustav Meyrink

Expressionism as Revolt, Jean-Michel Palmier

Benoit Misere, Leo Ferré

Nazi Bitches [author unknown]

The Four Ghosts [author unknown]

The Bit Between the Teeth, Vladimir Pozner

{ illegible }

A Cry in the Night, Arnold Golsworthy

The Life and Death of Atilla the Hun [author unknown]

Cha'Abba: His Life and Times, Lucien Louis Bellan

Check in Chess [author unknown]

Gurdjieff and the Holy Grail

Iranian Islam volume IV, Henry Corbin

The Angry Dead [author unknown]

Memoirs of a Revolutionary 1901-1941, Victor Serge

Triple Agent [author unknown]

The Devil [author unknown]

From Militia to Resistance, Bernard Delalande

The Executioner of Hearts, Mona Gloria

Gallery of Original Covers

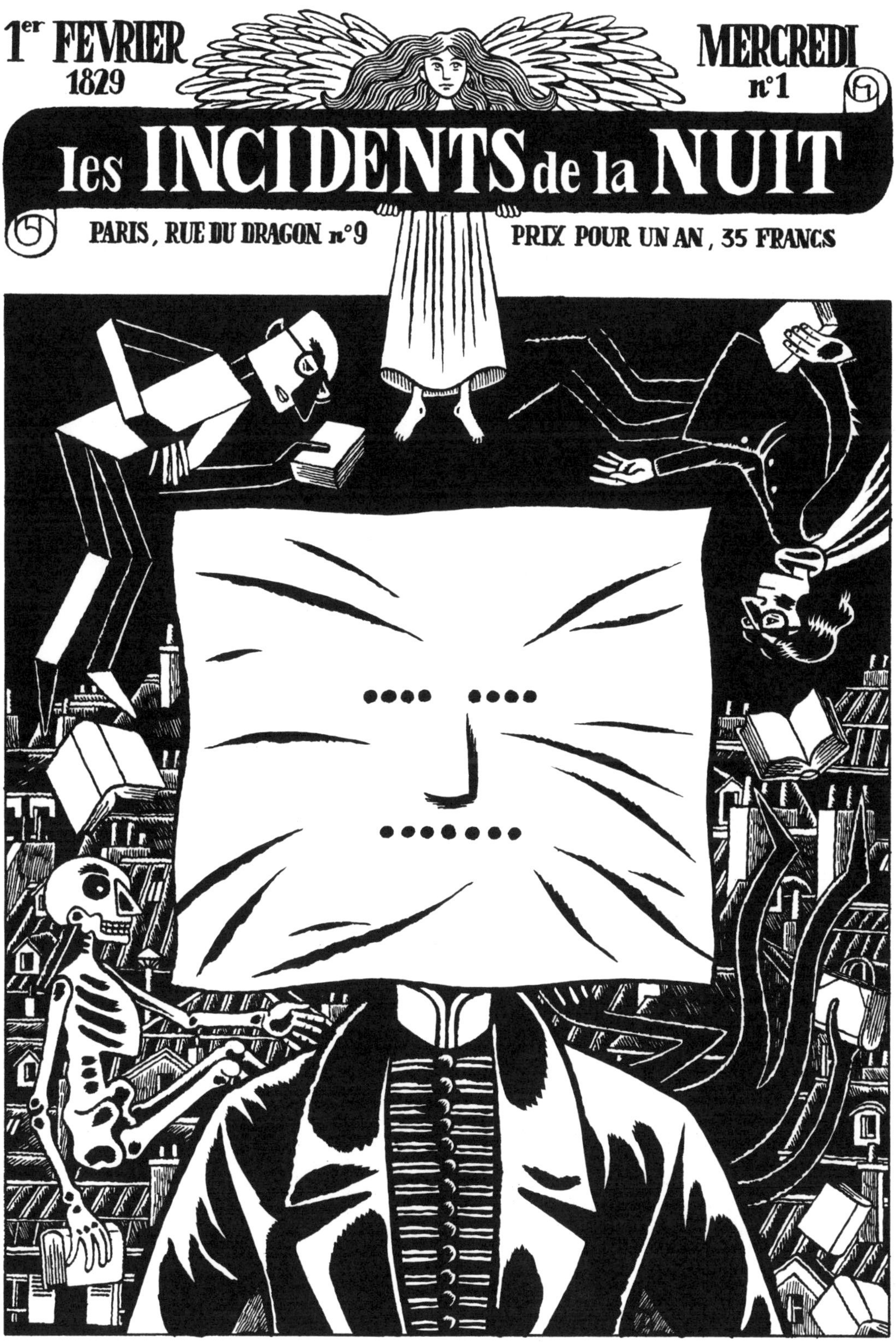
1er FEVRIER
1829
MERCREDI
n°1
les INCIDENTS de la NUIT
PARIS, RUE DU DRAGON n°9
PRIX POUR UN AN, 35 FRANCS

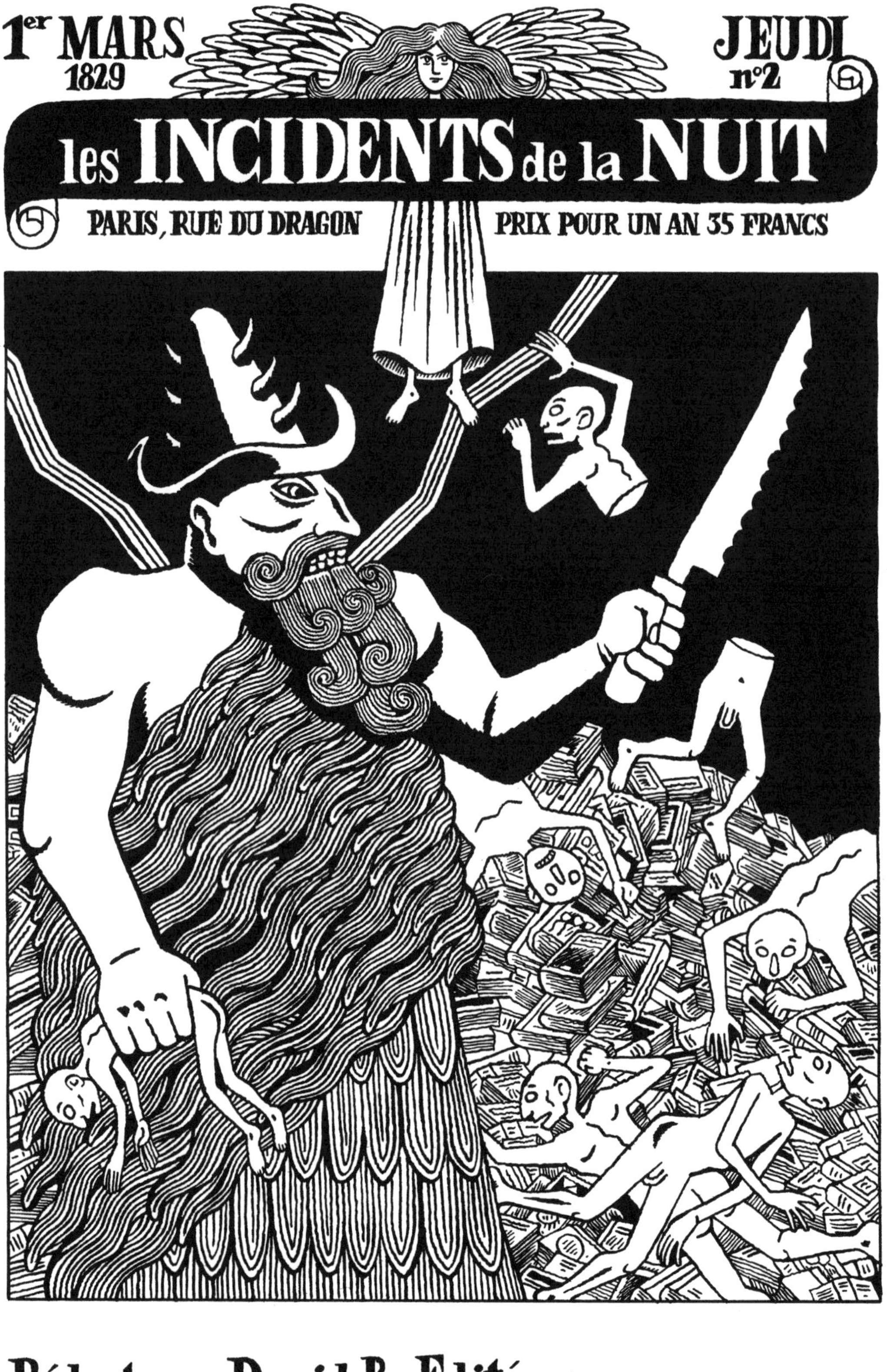
1er MARS
1829
JEUDI
n°2
les INCIDENTS de la NUIT
PARIS, RUE DU DRAGON
PRIX POUR UN AN 35 FRANCS

Rédacteur : David B . Edité par

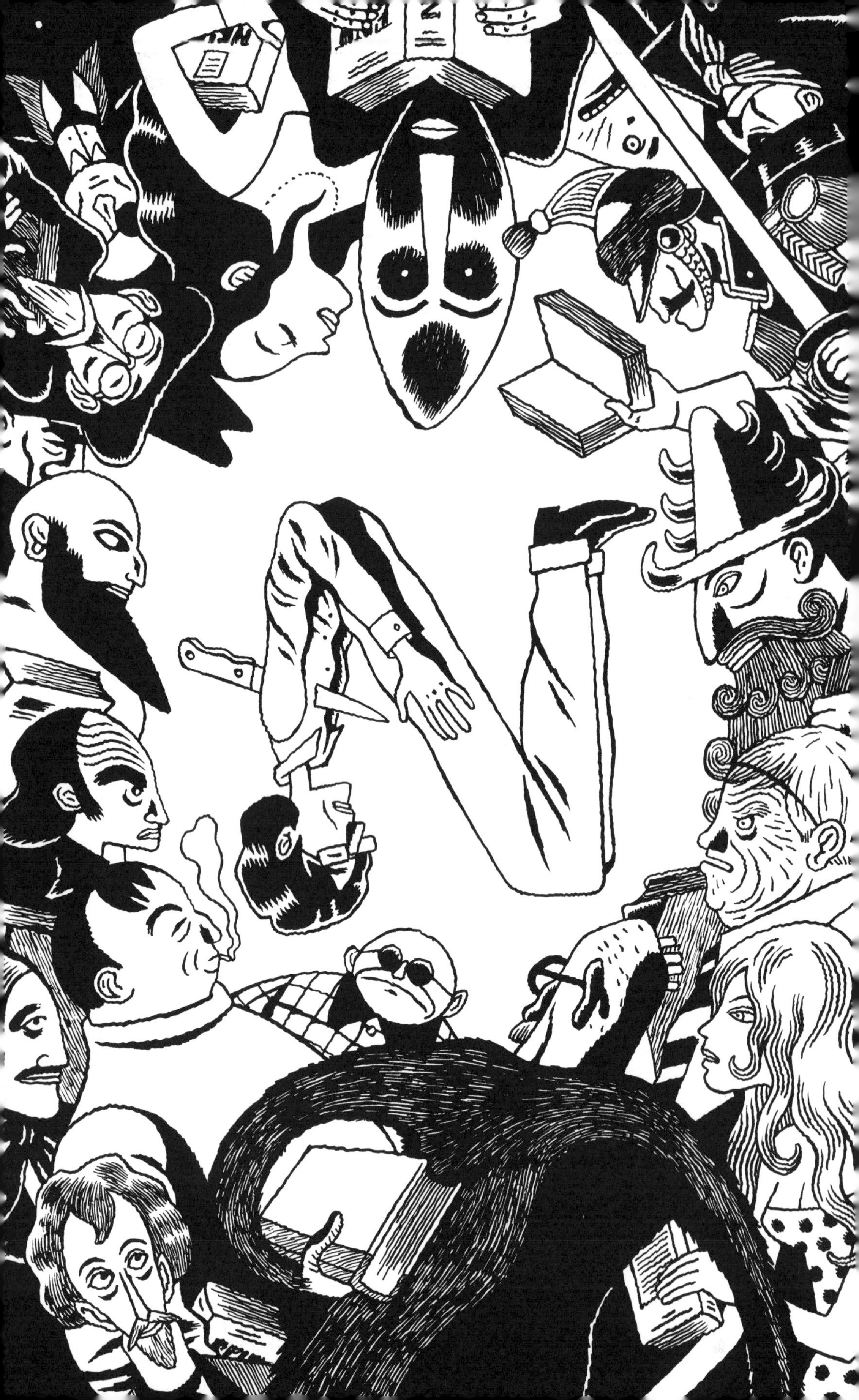

David B.

David B. is one of France's finest cartoonists and a co-founder of the
legendary L'Association collective. He is the author of many books
of comics including *The Armed Garden*, *Noctural Conspiracies*, and
Epileptic which was awarded Angoulême International Comics Festival
Prize for Scenario and the Ignatz Award for Outstanding Artist. He lives
and works in Paris, France.

Brian Evenson

Brian Evenson is the author of eleven prize-winning books of fiction, including *The Open Curtain*, *Last Days*, *Windeye*, and *Immobility*. His work has been translated into over a dozen languages. He lives and works in Providence, Rhode Island, where he teaches at Brown University.

Sarah Evenson

Sarah Evenson is also the co-translator of Manuela Draeger's *Belle-Medusa*. She lives and works in Minneapolis as a freelance illustrator. Visit her on the web at sarahevenson.tumblr.com.

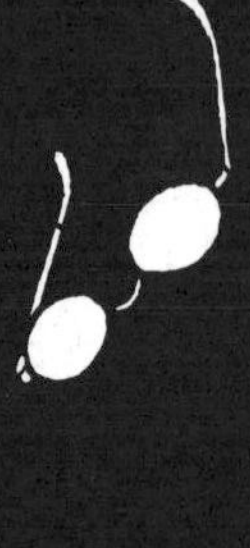